"Through the use of carefully crafted metaphors and analogies, Grassi shares authentic experiences that help us overcome obstacles, strengthen our character, and expand our faith. Recognized by some players as the Character Coach, Grassi offers many great ideas that will better prepare the reader to understand the sport of football and the game of life."

—Steve Wisniewski, 8-time All-Pro Guard, Oakland Raiders

"Jim Grassi explores the physical, mental, and spiritual sides of NFL players. *Crunch Time* is an enlightening experience that shows the true character of today's heroes of the gridiron."

—Mike Waufle, Defensive Line Coach, Oakland Raiders

CRUNCH TIME

JIM GRASSI

BETHANYHOUSE
PUBLISHERS
MINNEAPOLIS, MINNESOTA

Crunch Time
Copyright © 2002
Jim Grassi

Scripture credits and permissions are on page 6

Published by Bethany House Publishers
A Ministry of Bethany Fellowship International
11400 Hampshire Avenue South
Bloomington, Minnesota 55438
www.bethanyhouse.com

Printed in the United States of America

Library of Congress Cataloging-in-Publication Data

Grassi, James E., 1943-
    Crunch Time : what football can teach you about the game of life / by Jim Grassi
        p. cm.
Includes bibliographical references.
    ISBN 0-7642-2660-6 (hardback)
    1. Football—Anecdotes. 2. Football—Religious aspects—Christianity.
3. Christian life. 4. Conduct of life. I. Title.
    GV950.5 .G73   2002
    248.8'8—dc21   2002008648

Credits and Permissions

Dedication

Tom Landry was truly one of the great Americans of our time, one of the very few men who evoked the respect and the admiration of a nation. Behind that stoic expression and trademark profile stood a man full of passion to motivate people to reach their fullest potential. While striving to be the best at whatever he laid his hand to, he remained steadfast in his immovable character and his tremendous faith in God.

This book is dedicated to all coaches, players, team chaplains, and fans that aspire to uphold the ideals and values Coach Landry humbly modeled in his life. He left us with a wonderful legacy of what a *true disciple of Christ* looks like.

On September 11, 2001, thousands lost their lives in senseless acts of terrorism. To the courageous rescue workers, volunteers, and caregivers who modeled a *servant's heart* in the spirit of Coach Landry's legacy, we commend this work with the hope that it will inspire and encourage you to keep on keepin' on.

Acknowledgments

Great football is the result of dedication, perseverance, commitment, pride, poise, and teamwork. It has occurred to me that writing a book is similar, requiring many hours of research, planning, interviewing, and writing with the support and encouragement of a caring team of friends and acquaintances.

I especially wish to thank the Oakland Raiders and the San Francisco 49ers and their coaches and staff for all their cooperation and assistance in allowing me to observe behind-the-scenes activities that helped me with my research. These two fine organizations typify the professionalism and cooperation that now exist in the NFL.

Of particular encouragement were head coaches Jon Gruden, Bill Callahan, and Steve Mariucci, three of the most talented and dedicated men I've ever met. I also wish to acknowledge the special relationship and support God has given me through knowing the following men: Gary Anderson, Greg Biekert, Tim Brown, Jerome Davidson, Ginaro Denaoli, Norm Evans, Rich Gannon, Kevin Gogan, Tom Holmoe, Robert Jenkins, Brent Jones, Napoleon Kaufman, Tim Kohn, Jim Otto, Todd Petersen, Ryan Phillips, Jon Ritchie, Art Thoms, Coach Mike Waufle, and Steve Wisniewski. These men have not only imprinted me with their wonderful play but, more importantly, with their tremendous character.

This project would not have been possible without the constant love, support, and understanding of my beautiful bride of thirty-seven years. Thank you, Louise, for being my faithful partner. It is a true blessing to work together for God's kingdom.

I'm especially indebted to Bob and Stephanie Nelson, Geoff and Kristie Rinehart, and all my ministry partners, supporters, and board members who have faithfully served our twenty-two-year-old Let's Go Fishing Ministry. Also, Dr. Karen Hayter of Fort Worth, Texas, has provided me with enormous inspiration during the time I've known her. She is a gifted television host, counselor, writer, and sports fan, and she is truly committed to the principles found in God's Word. Thank you, Karen, for your support with this project.

As any author will tell you, the stress and strain attributed to enduring the twelve-hour days of sitting in one place without much exercise can create many problems with a previously injured back. Unfortunately, when I was playing sports, safety information or protective equipment were not priorities. The back injuries sustained in my youth continue to plague me, and without the assistance of an excellent physical therapist, chiropractor, and physician I would have been unable to endure those long, hard days at the computer. Thank you to Dynamic Rehab, to Dr. Tony Smith, and to Dr. Henry Downs.

Also, I wish to commend and thank the very gifted staff at Bethany House Publishers. Their amazing talents and enthusiasm have encouraged me to perfect and refine the concepts involved in this work. A special thank-you to my new teammate, Christopher Soderstrom. The faithful and constant prayer support of friends like Paul and Sandy Herrmann we felt throughout this project.

Finally: Thank you, Jesus!

Grow in the grace and knowledge of our Lord.

2 Peter 3:18 NASB

Contents

A Personal Message

Dear Friend,

I have been privileged to be involved with sports ministries for over twenty-two years. Through countless conferences, chapels, retreats, family camps, Special Kids Days for the disabled, single-parent programs, men's ministry events, and sportsmen's banquets, I have endeavored to present God's Word in a practical manner. The model I use in shaping my presentations is Jesus. Through the use of anecdotes, metaphors, and parables, I utilize real-life stories from my sports background and associations to help people focus on strengthening families and training disciples.

Let's Go Fishing Ministries is one of the oldest sports ministries in the country. It has served as a resource organization for churches and ministries wishing to impact their communities. Most recently we have embarked upon a vision to develop state-of-the-art multimedia presentations that assist others in developing dynamic programs on various sports themes. These presentations ultimately will be accessible through the Internet and will provide testimonials and technique demonstrations from some of the top Christian football players, hunters, fishermen, archers, and outdoorsmen in the world. The detailed format of program development and implementation will assist even the smallest fellowship in presenting a world-class program.

We call our new program *The Outdoor Connection Resources*. It is ideal for church community outreach events, conferences, men's ministry programs, women-of-the-wilderness meetings, youth rallies, and pastors' retreats. For more information on how you can access these resources, contact: Let's Go Fishing Ministries, P.O. Box 3303, Post Falls, ID 83877 or through our Web site: *www.letsgofishing.org*.

In His Service,
Jim Grassi

Foreword

—Steve Mariucci, Head Coach, San Francisco 49ers

During the past seven years I've been both inspired and supported by the personal counsel and writings of my friend Jim Grassi. His thought-provoking metaphors and biblical illustrations have helped shape my life, my family, and my faith.

By observing football from the inside out, Jim shares profound, life-changing stories that will deeply impact those who read *Crunch Time*. Through locker-room conversations and personal relationships with many coaches and athletes, he has developed insights that help build lasting character.

Football continues to grow in its popularity. With increased success come great expectations for both athletes and coaches to perform at superhuman levels. This can produce tremendous stress and emotional conflict, sometimes resulting in behaviors that ultimately disgrace the sport and the individual.

Our newspapers and sports programs are filled with sad stories of a few players who have made tragic errors in judgment. However, most successful athletes desire to establish a positive reputation both on and off the field. Jim Grassi's writings and messages have helped many coaches and athletes to work on becoming better persons, and resources like *Crunch Time* will help all of us to work through those challenging obstacles and temptations that life brings.

I've had the privilege of coaching championship teams at both the college and professional levels. I'm convinced that the athletes who consistently perform at the highest level are the ones who have discovered many of the spiritual truths and character-building principles spelled out in this book.

To many players and coaches, Jim Grassi is known as our *Character Coach*. To me, Jim is a mentor and friend who seeks to serve God by unselfishly sharing his life with others. *Crunch Time* is a must-read for anyone interested in football, faith, and building strong character.

Chapter

Countdown to Kickoff

Concentration is all-important. And the key is to concentrate your way through the bad times.

—Dan Fouts

Hall-of-Fame Charger Quarterback

> **"I** never made the team.... I was not heavy enough to play the line, not fast enough to play halfback, and not smart enough to be a quarterback."
>
> —Richard Nixon

1

Quarterbacking the Game of Life

In 1980 Jets QB Richard Todd completed 42 throws against the 49ers, setting an NFL record. In 1984 Dan Marino completed 48 TD passes and gained 5,084 yards for the Miami Dolphins. Steve Young proved himself worthy to be considered one of the best ever when he threw 6 TDs in the 49ers' victory over the San Diego Chargers in Super Bowl XXIX. Great quarterbacks, all.

The 2000 campaign unveiled the multifaceted talents of a well-traveled veteran quarterback named Rich Gannon. Before taking the helm for the Oakland Raiders, Gannon was a backup signal caller for Kansas City, Washington, and Minnesota. Through much adversity he persevered and perfected his game, developing his extraordinary abilities to anticipate the blitz, run with the ball, and complete critical passes. Gannon's development has made winners of the Oakland Raiders.

As I study first-rate quarterbacks and survey literature on their position, it seems that Tom Bass was correct in his analysis of the "playmakers." In his book *Play Football the NFL Way*, he tells us there are four critical elements to being a successful passer:

1. The *set* is the quarterback's drop-back. A good plant on his back foot is critical in transferring his momentum into his throwing arm.

2. The *forward step* shifts the QB's direction and directs his energy toward his receiver.

3. The *release* or *delivery* is the most critical stage. The "hips of the player should open up and be square with the receiver." The QB should throw the ball with "the trunk of his body and not merely his arm."

4. The body's *follow-through* after releasing the ball is fundamental to the pass's final outcome.

The steps needed for having a solid relationship with God are much like the elements mentioned above. We must *set* our minds and hearts in a new direction by first stopping the backward slide of negative character flaws that bring us to sin. The *forward step* is important as we begin to move toward God's plan for our life. As we open up and become square with Him, our spirit is *released* for service; He sees our heart and forgives us for our past failures. Finally, we must commit to the *follow-through*—if we are sincere, there should be a change of heart, a change of attitude, and a change of actions, reflecting God's Spirit and love within us.

Let's strongly compete for those who are lost and for those who haven't perfected the skills of being a Christlike Christian. Let's make sure our grip on life is firm. And most importantly, let's keep on working toward perfecting those character traits that glorify God.

Now change your mind and attitude to God and turn to him so he can cleanse away your sins and send you wonderful times of refreshment from the presence of the Lord.

—*Acts 3:19* TLB

"I was scared. I thought Detroit was going to draft me. I was going to ask for so much money that they'd have to put me on layaway."

—Deion Sanders

2

Your Name Is on the Back

What legacy would you like to leave to your family and colleagues after finishing your career? Recognizing that the average NFL player's career lasts about three years, it is important that a player properly embraces and protects each and every moment in order to guard his reputation.

Disgrace and scandals fill the headlines of our daily newspapers. Reporters seem to revel in broadcasting the moral failures of prominent people, especially those connected with professional sports. Hypocrisy prevails as people adopt an attitude of arrogance.

Should a professional football player be expected to maintain a higher standard of conduct than the average worker? NFL Commissioner Paul Tagliabue and many head coaches suggest that there is an agreed-upon code of conduct for the professional athlete. However, an epidemic of player arrests for offenses ranging from drunk driving to sexual assault to murder reflects poorly on the league and its teams. Even though discussions about intervention programs and increased discipline continue, teams must find a way to balance the risk by helping players stay within accepted moral bounds.

Dave Wannstedt of the Miami Dolphins states, "Character is something that is at the top of our list on draft day." Recently I spoke with a head coach who said, "I spend 80 percent of my time trying to work through problems with a small group of thugs who if they weren't playing NFL football would probably be in jail. That means I don't have enough time left to work with the players who would both benefit from and appreciate timely counsel and advice."

What is character? *Character is the moral, ethical, and spiritual undergirding—resting on truth—that reinforces a life and resists the temptation to compromise.* Character is doing the right thing on purpose, doing the right thing regardless of the consequences.

I've had the privilege of working with a few teams in the area of character development. I regularly ask players to consider their reputation and the legacy they wish to leave when their pro ball days are over. Most of them haven't taken the time to think about the question of how they will be remembered beyond their physical abilities.

I endeavor to explain the importance of leaving football with a positive image, one that won't soil their family name. A proverb reminds us, "A good name is to be more desired than great riches" (Proverbs 22:1 NASB). The next generation will not remember the ranking of a player as much as they will recall his attitudes and comments made in front of the camera or how he lived his personal and family life.

When giving a talk on character to athletes I often ask them to silently answer the following questions:

Quiz 1

- Who are the five wealthiest people in the world?
- Who are the last five Heisman Trophy winners?
- Who are five people who have received a Nobel or Pulitzer Prize?
- Who are the last six Best Actor Academy Award winners?

Quiz 2

- Name five coaches or teachers who were instrumental in helping you get to this level.
- Name three people in your life who have stood beside you during difficult times.
- Name someone who has made you feel worthy and appreciated.
- Name three heroes whose lives have inspired you.

Not one person can provide correct answers for every question posed in Quiz 1. However, everyone has complete answers for Quiz 2. The conclusion reached is that people who make the greatest difference in life aren't the ones with the most fortune, the most fame, the most power, or the most credentials. The ones who have the greatest impact are people of good character. The life-changers are the people who inspire and encourage us to be successful first and foremost as a person.

More important than an individual's physical skills, more important than his game preparation, more important than his knowledge of football, more important than his leadership abilities, and more important than his ability to coach others, is the development of great character. Character is also the single most consistent quality for success in life.

Part of character is doing our very best all the time. As one farmer put it, "Leave the woodpile a little higher than you found it." One of the toughest jobs a coach has is creating a good work ethic among prima-donna players. On every team there are a few players who still think they're on scholarship and that they only need to show up to be revered and praised. However, today's game requires everyone, even the more gifted players, to develop a personal work ethic that encourages them and their team members to achieve a higher level of play. True champions mold this trait into their character.

People often compromise their integrity today because they operate from a mindset of following the crowd: they listen more to others than to God. They are more concerned with "being like them" than "being like Him." When Christ delivered His Sermon on the Mount, one purpose was to communicate what is required for godly character (to be like Him). Jesus encouraged His followers to be of good virtue and to act out of a pure heart. If we are to be the "salt of the earth" and the "light of the world," we need to follow Christ's teachings.

I've found that when I take responsibility for my character, the X's and O's of my life fall into place; when I don't, they fall apart. I hope that when the game of life is over, my friends and family will remember me as a man of good and strong character.

He has showed you, O man, what is good. And what does the Lord require of you? To act justly and to love mercy and to walk humbly with your God.

—Micah 6:8

3

Patience: A Key to Success

One of the main attributes of a successful quarterback is enormous patience. It takes patience (and trust) to wait in the pocket until one of your receivers finally breaks open. It takes patience to know that in the two-minute drill at the end of a close game there is still plenty of time to move up the field and score. Patience is needed in attacking a defense after your team has received a ten-yard penalty for holding. A patient quarterback will not try to move the ball twenty yards in one play if the pass seems too risky. He will use two or three plays that have a higher probability of success in obtaining the necessary yardage.

When Steve Young rode the bench for several years behind Joe Montana, he had to be patient. As mentioned, Rich Gannon was a backup QB for several teams before his day in the sun with the Raiders. All-Pro Kurt Warner languished through many years of semi-pro ball, arena ball, and the European League before he had his shot in the NFL. Johnny Unitas had to wait patiently for his undersized body to catch up with his playmaking mind.

Patience is truly a great virtue in professional football. Waiting for the right opportunity to take advantage of a break might mean the difference between success and failure. Outside of a person's family and faith, few things can take the place of patience. Talent will not do it—nothing is more common than unsuccessful men with talent. Genius will not do it—unrewarded brilliance is almost a proverb. Patience and determination alone are of supreme importance.

Recently I was reading a devotional book called *Strength for Today* by Dr. John MacArthur. His insightful comments on how the apostle Paul patiently dealt with struggles bear repeating. Paul's letter to the Ephesians was written to encourage the new believers and remind them to be thankful for God's immeasurable blessings. Paul's challenge to suffering servants was to be patient with those who attack us.

In our instant, microwave, drive-through, I-want-it-now culture, patience is hard to come by. We get anxious waiting five seconds for our computer screen to organize itself. We change lines at the supermarket if we see more than three people ahead of us. We are a driven society, and with that we get more and more opportunities for misunderstandings, inappropriate conclusions, and losses of temper.

God's Word tells us that mature believers are marked by patience. In the Greek, *patience* is defined as being "long-tempered" or "long-suffering." In Scripture, we see at least three aspects of biblical patience that should encourage every reader.

First, patience never gives in to negative circumstances, no matter how difficult. God told Abraham He would make him into a great nation and give the Promised Land to his descendants (Genesis 12:2, 7). When God made this promise, Abraham and Sarah had no children. They had to wait far beyond childbearing years before God gave them a son. But Hebrews 6:15 (NASB) says, "Having patiently waited, [Abraham] obtained the promise." He did not waver but focused upon the assurances of God. Where is our focus today? On our problems, or on the words of truth?

A *second* part of patience is coping with difficult people. Professional football is not much different from public administration, business, or ministry. Personalities don't always mix, management styles differ, expectations vary, and misunderstandings occur. The nature of the pressures and stressors in life can produce friction. Paul tells us to "be patient with all men" (1 Thessalonians 5:14 NASB), especially those of the "household of faith." This is gentleness, grace, and mercy, especially for those who share our belief in Jesus.

Finally, patience accepts God's plan for everything. A patient person says, "We know that God causes all things to work together for good to those who love God, to those who are called according to His purpose" (Romans 8:28 NASB). This is a reminder to all of us that since God is in control, we can be patient, waiting for Him to work out His will. If we are having problems with wanting to control things, maybe we need to give it all to Jesus! Let's try to remember the lessons on patience from God's Word.

Friends, as an example of patience in the face of suffering, take the apostle's words that he spoke in the name of the Lord: "As you know, we consider blessed those who have persevered. You have heard of Job's perseverance and have seen what the Lord finally brought about. The Lord is full of compassion and mercy. Above all, my brothers, do not swear—not by heaven or by earth or by anything else. Let your 'Yes' be yes, and your 'No,' no, or you will be condemned" (James 5:10–12).

Therefore, as God's chosen people, holy and dearly loved, clothe yourselves with compassion, kindness, humility, gentleness and patience.
—Colossians 3:12

> **"T**he harder you work, the harder it is to surrender."
>
> —Vince Lombardi, Former Packers Coach

4

Coaching to Win

I really enjoy watching coaches interact with their players. You can spot the great teachers because they are encouragers. Having attended a few training camps, I've been privileged to see two of the NFL's best coaches—Tampa Bay's Jon Gruden (then with Oakland) and San Francisco's Steve Mariucci. As you leaf through their teams' media guides you will find that these young leaders have already set numerous individual coaching records.

What is the key to their success? While hard work, dedication, raw intelligence, leadership skills, and football knowledge all play a critical part in developing their successful records, the most visible asset is their ability to motivate their teams with the proper use of encouragement. Both coaches are well known for their unique enthusiasm, often manifested in curious facial expressions. They are also known for the confidence they impart to players through their contagious encouragement. The words "good job," "way to go," "you make me proud," "I like what I see," and other such affirming expressions regularly echo from the sideline to each player who demonstrates pure talent or who makes a good decision. Most players will tell you that a coach's timely advice, counsel, suggestion, or critique—provided in an encouraging way—will lift them up and cause them to continue playing with more determination.

In his book *The Power of Encouragement*, Pastor David Jeremiah of Shadow Mountain Church in El Cajon, California, explains what it means to encourage others from a biblical perspective:

> Each of us lives some of our days in the war zone! Weekly we face battles, challenges, and shock. When we see the missiles flying overhead, we need someone who will give us encouragement. Encouragement is transfusing some of your courage into another life.

The Bible says, "In the last days perilous times will come" (1 Timothy 3:1 NKJV). The book of Hebrews says we ought to be more and more involved in encouragement as these days approach. When the perilous times increase and the battles intensify, we will need encouragement more than ever.

One of the motivations behind Paul's letters to the New Testament churches was his desire to encourage those who faced life-threatening challenges every day. In the beginning verses of almost every one of his letters, Paul's priority message was a word of hope and affirmation.

There's no such thing as a person who doesn't need encouragement. The one who seems perfectly capable and well put together is often the one who needs it the most. Timely words of encouragement not only produce winning football teams but also people who are filled with comfort and understanding. God also wants us to encourage ourselves with His truth and with the loving grace of the Holy Spirit.

Preach the Word; be prepared in season and out of season; correct, rebuke and encourage—with great patience and careful instruction.
—2 Timothy 4:2

> "Gentlemen, nothing funny ever happened on a football field."
>
> —Tom Landry

5

Building a Legacy

While I never had the opportunity to personally meet Coach Tom Landry, I know well of his character and reputation. We were both a part of the Fellowship of Christian Athletes, and many of my Dallas Theological Seminary friends who knew him well often spoke of his great faith.

There are many who would consider this recently deceased coach as one of the most admired and revered men in professional sports. In Bob St. John's book titled *Landry: The Legend and the Legacy*, many of Landry's personal character traits, football successes, and spiritual experiences are discussed in detail. The testimonies of several prominent people connected with football help us to understand what made up this successful man. If you desire to have a great legacy, the following attributes identified by those who knew Landry well could be placed on the top of your list.

> *He was the classiest act in coaching . . . a great coach but a greater man. . . . I loved him for what he meant in my life and what he meant to the game.*
>
> —Mike Ditka, Former Bears Coach

> *He taught me to take the heat; just stand up and face it. . . . He gave me great confidence when I could have lost it. When he did that, he got me for life. I would*

have run through a brick wall for him. He had such patience and insight into human nature.

—Charlie Waters, Former Dallas Cowboy

Tom Landry had a decency about him that was unsurpassed.... He did things for the right reasons. That's what his Christian religion taught him to do ... the right thing.

—Roger Staubach, Hall-of-Fame Cowboy

I don't need to be in the Hall of Fame or Ring of Honor to punctuate my career. What counts ... more than anything is that I played eleven years for Coach Tom Landry. You can't get any more respect than that.

—Drew Pearson, Former Dallas Cowboy

Landry's legacy is one of towering achievements, modest demeanor, discipline, teamwork, straight talk, loyalty, commitment, and faith.

—Paul Tagliabue, NFL Commissioner

Coach Landry was the best representative the game could offer. From the glory years of contending Super Bowl teams through the dog days at the end of his career, he was consistently a gentleman and a committed man of God. When the team's new owner fired the "world's favorite coach," a seismic shock was set off in Dallas. People felt betrayed and abandoned as football lost a great leader and friend.

I believe that a little of America's goodness died with the passing of Tom Landry in February 2000. The coach was once quoted as saying,

> As a model for my approach to athletes I think of Abraham, the Old Testament patriarch. His greatness was found in his hospitality to strangers (Genesis 18:1–8), his obedience to God (Genesis 26:5), and the blessing of the Lord upon his family and his life (Genesis 24:1).

He went on to say,

> My encouragement to football players is to develop a Christlike character. I remind them that the greatest honor is not playing in a Super Bowl or being inducted into the Hall of Fame but having their name used to describe God the Father.

The legacy of this great coach provides a wonderful role model for each of us. If you follow the example of Tom Landry, you will have a Christlike life.

Scripture refers to the Lord as "the God of Abraham" (Genesis 26:24 KJV). What an honor! There is no greater reward or tribute for a person than to have the God of all creation call him His friend. In three separate places in God's Word we see Abraham called a "friend of God." Abraham's example of love, respect, obedience, faithfulness, and praise should inspire each of us to become known as God's friend. Coach Tom Landry certainly was.

But you, O Israel, my servant, Jacob, whom I have chosen, you descendants of Abraham my friend . . .

—*Isaiah 41:8*

> **"H**e's so short his breath smells of earthworms."
>
> —**Ron Meyer,** Former SMU Coach,
> on 5'9" Guard Harvey McAtee

6

The Underdog

W hile many might have differing opinions as to what was the greatest comeback victory in NFL history, you won't get much of an argument from those who attended the 1992 playoff game between the Houston Oilers and the Buffalo Bills at Rich Stadium in Buffalo. The Bills had played a miserable half of football and were behind the Oilers by a score of 35–3. If "Dandy" Don Meredith had been announcing the game, he would have broken into his chorus, "Turn out the lights, the party's over."

Things were not going well for the Bills' quarterback, Frank Reich, who was starting his first NFL playoff game. Despite being effective during the regular season, the Bills' offense just couldn't get anything going. As the whistle blew to begin the third quarter, Reich started to think about a song he'd listened to several times the preceding week. In fact, he'd written down the lyrics just that morning. It was *In Christ Alone*, written by Shawn Craig and Don Koch and sung by Michael English. While no NFL team had ever come back from a 32-point deficit in a playoff game, his faith and confidence remained strong as he reflected on the words of that inspiring song.

The commentators viewing the game called it "nothing short of a miracle." Frank Reich led the Bills to an overtime victory of 41–38. Despite the media's attention being focused on the remarkable victory, God had other plans for the post-game press conference. Reich pulled out the lyrics from *In Christ Alone* and read to the assembled crowd the words that testified to the great faith and perseverance that he and his teammates demonstrated.

Just a few weeks later Reich again reviewed the comforting words from this song as he and his teammates picked up the pieces after a crushing 52–17 loss to the Cowboys in Super Bowl XXVII. The message he heard gave him a new insight: "It's not that we can experience victory in *all* our circumstances, but that Christ gives us the strength and hope to overcome all odds. We need to learn that God helps us deal with life in a positive manner—even when you lose a Super Bowl."

When I think of stories of hope, perseverance, and teamwork, I'm reminded of a story about a Special Olympics held in Seattle a few years ago. Nine contestants, all physically or mentally disabled, assembled at the starting line for the 100-yard dash. At the gun, they all started out, not exactly in a dash but with a relish to run the race to the finish and win—all, that is, except one little boy who stumbled on the asphalt, tumbled over a couple of times, and began to weep.

The other eight heard the boy cry. They slowed down and looked back, then they all turned around and headed for the starting line—every one of them. One girl with Down's syndrome bent down and kissed him on the forehead and said, "This will make it better." Then all nine linked arms and walked together to the finish line.

Everyone in the stadium stood, and the cheering went on for several minutes. People who were there are still telling the story. Why? Because deep down they knew this one thing: What matters in this life is more than winning for ourselves. What matters is helping others to win, even if it means slowing down and changing our course.

The apostle Paul reminds us, "Do not merely look out for your own personal interests, but also for the interests of others" (Philippians 2:4 NASB). God wants us to have a serious, caring involvement in some of the goals others are concerned about. One way this can happen is to take our eyes off ourselves and think about how we can effectively love, serve, and encourage others.

Carry each other's burdens, and in this way you will fulfill the law of Christ.

—Galatians 6:2

"I wasn't much good. When I went into the line on a fake, I would holler, 'I don't have it!' "

—**Bob Newhart**, Comedian,
on his high school career

7

Keep Your Eyes on the Ball

How often have you heard a commentator or a coach talk about a player missing a catch or handoff because he took his eyes off the ball? A good receiver "looks the ball" into his hand—his gaze is so fixed on the spiraling leather that a defender hitting him seems like a distant possibility. With a similar focus the running back charges to the line of scrimmage, relying upon the quarterback's eyes and timing to carefully spot the ball into the pocket created with the runner's arms.

It is critical to the ultimate success of a football player to have excellent hand-eye coordination. Even defensive linemen have their special eyes-on-the-ball drill in order to help them become better focused. Mike Waufle, defensive line coach for the Oakland Raiders, utilizes a painted green football connected to a long string as an aid to help his linemen focus on the ball's movement. As he snatches the grass-colored ball from the turf, the linemen must carefully time their charge with any motion in it. "I like to see my linemen so focused on ball movement that they rivet their attention on the very tip of the ball," he says. "Usually a player will pick up that the ball is being snapped when the tip of the ball begins to move."

This split-second difference in a lineman picking up the snap can make the difference in delivering the attack or waiting for it to come to him. A lineman's catlike quickness can be a positive factor only when he fixes his gaze on the ball.

During the three-plus years Jesus spent with His disciples, they witnessed many miracles. The apostle Peter was particularly impressed as he watched his Savior walk toward him on water. His immediate response was, "Lord, if it's you, tell me to come to you" (Matthew 14:28). Peter was a lot like many of us—impulsively direct! He wanted to step out in faith and be with Jesus.

Jesus said, "Come." Peter *fixed his gaze upon the Lord* and stepped onto the water. He did not walk around the boat or head off to a better fishing hole; he walked straight toward Jesus. What happened next to Peter is the same thing that happens to all of us when we take our focus off the Master—we sink, or in football vernacular, we fumble the handoff or drop the pass or mistime the snap: "But when [Peter] saw the wind, he was afraid and, beginning to sink, cried out, 'Lord, save me!' " (14:30).

Peter broke contact with Jesus the moment his gaze became fixated on the wind and the waves. Just like a receiver who becomes distracted with a defensive back closing in on him, his concentration was broken. Once we place our attention outside the object of our focus, we risk missing an opportunity to be successful.

When we are truly centered upon the Lord with our prayerful life, our worship, and our actions, He will handle our problems and help conquer our fears. The Holy Spirit makes us strong and able to walk boldly and with confidence (Proverbs 3:26). As we keep focused on Jesus, all else in our lives will be seen in proper perspective with less chance of a major fumble. No problem is too big—for He is always with us.

You have the option of catching it by either end.

—*Johnny Unitas,*
on Billy Kilmer's wobbly passes

"There are a thousand reasons for failure but not a single excuse."

—**Mike Reid,** Former Bengal Lineman

8

Can the Devil Make Me Do It?

Sorting through some of the discouraging headlines from the *USA Today* Sports section, I find an amazing number of columns dealing exclusively with the topic of character, or lack thereof.

- "Character Complicates Choices" (April 12, 2000)
- "Teams Must Weigh Talent Against Off-the-Field Personality" (April 12, 2000)
- "Lewis Pleads to Lesser Charge, Avoids Jail Time" (June 6, 2000)
- "Accused BYU Cornerback to Sit" (June 6, 2000)
- "Chmura Cut by Packers—Awaits Sex Trial" (June 6, 2000)
- "Broncos' Romanowski Indicted" (August 10, 2000)
- "Irvin Arrested on Marijuana Charges" (August 10, 2000)

And the beat goes on . . . and on . . . and on.

Paul Tagliabue recently stated that there is a "crisis of character in the NFL." Good character is more important than terrific times in the 40-yard dash or great moves in the open field. NFL teams can't afford to ignore the importance of character when rating the potential of a prospective player.

Dan Reeves guided the 1998 Atlanta Falcons through an amazing Cinderella season culminating with a chance to win a championship at Super

Bowl XXXIII in January 1999. Many felt the momentum was in favor of the Falcons as they endeavored to take on a very tough Denver Broncos squad. Eugene Robinson had already won a Super Bowl ring with the Green Bay Packers and was recruited by Reeves to assist the Falcons with their history-making charge into the record books. Not only was Robinson a multitalented defensive back, but he was also a tremendous leader and positive role model for the team.

But on the evening preceding the big game, after receiving an award celebrating his character, he let his guard down and surrendered to the temptation of requesting sex from a prostitute. As a married man and a Christian, he knew better. Despite having his family in town for the game, Eugene made a mistake that not only soiled his fine reputation but also put his team into a tailspin. Robinson was arrested for soliciting an undercover police-woman. After spending the night in jail, he was bailed out in time for pre-game practice.

Newspaper columnists and television comedians suggested "the devil made him do it." Others tried to excuse his actions by saying, "He's only a guy with a normal sex drive." Some close to Robinson testified that the temptations facing a good-looking athlete are ever-present and sometimes impossible to resist. Nothing anyone could say, however, would restore his good name and ease the anguish caused to his family. Robinson learned a painful lesson from his indiscretion. No one is exempt from falling into temptation if they let their guard down.

If we identify fully with what it means to be a true disciple of Christ, if we submit ourselves totally to God's authority over everything, if we humbly wish to serve Him in all our endeavors, then we will find ourselves in direct conflict with Satan. There is no room to compromise with the Evil One.

We are either aligned with the kingdom of God and His lordship over our lives, or we are in Satan's kingdom and under his control. It is impossible to serve two masters. We cannot expect to play in the arena with evil elements and effectively work for the Lord. Anyone who possesses spiritual humility will take an uncompromising stand against anything that doesn't glorify Him. To "resist the devil" means "to take a stand against" the person of Satan and anything he represents. It's like President George W. Bush said regarding terrorism: "Either a nation is against terrorism, or by the fact that they don't take a position they are for the support of terrorism."

Prior to being Christians, we didn't have a problem with temptation, but if you are a believer, you have a new life in Christ. As the apostle Paul states,

"You were dead in your trespasses and sins, in which you formerly walked according to the course of this world, according to the prince of the power of the air [Satan]" (Ephesians 2:1–2 NASB).

Prior to accepting Christ into your life you had little power to resist Satan's pull. Our leveling influences were societal laws, cultural morals, our upbringing, and those people who influenced our decisions (family, friends, etc.).

Now, however, as people of deep convictions and having solid faith in Jesus Christ, we have a more powerful influence in our lives, the Holy Spirit. If we appropriate God's power to stand firm and resist the temptations that life brings, He will provide a way out for us. I'm reminded of the verse that kept me out of a great deal of trouble in my youth: "No temptation has seized you except what is common to man. And God is faithful; he will not let you be tempted beyond what you can bear. But when you are tempted, he will also provide a way out so that you can stand up under it" (1 Corinthians 10:13).

What temptations do you face? Are you humbly seeking God in your daily walk? We are called upon to flee from Satan's influence and humble ourselves before the Lord. Being humble before God doesn't mean being weak before Satan. Seek the Lord, and He will enable you to stand firm.

Resist the devil, and he will flee from you.

—*James 4:7* NASB

9

Controlled Chaos

In 1996 the chaplain of the California Bears college football team and its then head coach, Steve Mariucci, invited me to present a message to the team before their Saturday game. As is my custom, I arrived early to check out the surroundings and to have some quiet time before being introduced.

Much to my surprise, the first group to appear was Coach Mariucci and several of his assistant coaches. After introducing himself, he told me that chapel was an important part of his team's pregame preparation, and he encouraged all his players to attend.

Shortly after my message, Mariucci and I discussed the importance of spending regular time reading God's Word and being encouraged by others. Before leaving for the game, I promised to provide him weekly with some type of inspirational message. In order to properly prepare these spiritual vignettes, I endeavored to become acquainted with the type of pressures and concerns facing men in his position.

At the end of that exciting season, Mariucci was invited to be the head coach for the San Francisco 49ers. The pressure of being one of the league's youngest head coaches, coupled with the chaos in the front office, proved to be a real challenge for this gifted man. Since 1997 the 49ers have struggled through salary cap problems, the retirement of superstar players, the owner of the team being forced to leave football, and a legacy with the fans that has defined failure as not getting to the Super Bowl.

However, even with all that pressure, Mariucci's faith, abilities, talent, and patience provided the ingredients needed to survive. The 2001 season began. Salary cap purgatory made it so that the 49ers had to cut some of their very best players before the season even started. The front-office struggles and power plays led to speculation that this would be his last season. All-Pro receiver Terrell Owens continued to test the coach's patience and provided plenty of fodder for the media. After the gifted receiver dropped a potential game-winning pass against the Chicago Bears, he alleged that the reason the 49ers lost was that Mariucci wasn't going all out to beat his friend, Chicago Coach Dick Jauron.

All this plus being regularly challenged and reviewed by consultant and former coach Bill Walsh places an enormous amount of responsibility on a coach. But despite all the craziness and headaches, Coach Mariucci led his team into the playoffs again.

What is it that empowers a man to endure the trials of being a head coach? How can a person survive the onslaught of the combined pressure from prima-donna players, front-office demands, community scrutiny, and family needs? The great collegiate coach Lou Holtz once said this about the uncertainties of his profession: "One day you're drinking wine, and the next day you're picking the grapes."

President Harry Truman had a solid insight on the unique pressures of coaching: "It's a lot tougher to be a football coach than a president. You've got four years as president, and they guard you. A coach doesn't have anyone to protect him when things go wrong."

The enduring owners and fans of the past have been replaced with demands for instant success from coaches who have yet to gain the wisdom and experience that only trials and tribulation can bring. Would the media and fans of today be patient and visionary during the tough times that it took to shape great coaches like George Halas, Paul Brown, Weeb Ewbank, Vince Lombardi, and Tom Landry?

Today we recognize coaches like Steve Mariucci by their ability to effectively manage chaos and confusion. They must be multitalented in all aspects of the game and be able to select and manage outstanding position coaches that can effectively communicate and motivate their players to get the job done. Coaches like Mariucci are difficult to find and harder to keep. They possess unique capabilities to remain in control and poised even during times of personal attack.

In Gene Getz's wonderful book *The Measure of a Man*, he discusses what it takes to be a man of God. His thoughts about the apostle Paul are fascinating to contemplate. Paul commended those who wish to lead: "It is a fine work he desires to do" (1 Timothy 3:1 NASB). But he further explained that we should make sure that we are a certain kind of person. We must be beyond reproach, temperate, self-controlled, respectable, gentle, and able to manage our families.

Paul said the same thing to Titus as he sought to appoint leaders in Crete. In the same way you pick a good coach, Paul got beyond the generalities of "he's a good guy" or "I like his personality." Paul shows us specific characteristics that are marks of a man of God.

Getz also tells us that these characteristics are shaped and formed during trials and tribulations *over a period of time*. The measure of God's man begins by refining and perfecting the following traits in our lives:

- above reproach
- husband of one wife
- temperate
- prudent
- respectable
- hospitable
- able to teach
- not [given to drunkenness]
- not pugnacious
- not contentious
- gentle
- free from the love of money
- manages his own household well
- not a new convert
- not conceited
- has a good reputation with those outside the church
- not rebellious
- not self-willed
- not quick-tempered
- loves what is good
- sensible

- just
- devout
- self-controlled
  (1 Timothy 3:2–7; Titus 1:6–8 NASB)

I like the way Gene Getz sums up the list:

> A man of God, then, does not "suddenly appear." It takes time to become like Jesus Christ—a process, of course, which is not complete until we are with Him. But there is a definite level of spiritual maturity that is discernible, both by the individual who is evaluating his own life as well as those who associate with him.

The logical question for someone wishing to become a better person is "Where do I begin?" The answer is to take each of these characteristics, understand what they mean, and set out in a direction to refine your character hour by hour and day by day to incorporate a Christlike character.

◀▦▶

God does not grade on a curve; do right at all times.
—Lou Holtz, South Carolina Coach

Chapter

Kickoff

Pro football might be mankind's most highly publicized human endeavor.

—David Hill

President, Sports Division, Fox Network

> "**P**ro football is like nuclear warfare. There are no winners—only survivors."
>
> —Frank Gifford

10

In the Beginning

Long before Cris Carter, Tim Brown, and Jerry Rice were born, many players and coaches paved the way for these superstars to excel in one of America's favorite sports. From very obscure beginnings, on November 6, 1869, a half-century before there was an NFL, two teams—from Rutgers and Princeton—played what historians consider the first college football game.

The game resembled a soccer or rugby game more than what we now categorize as football. The rules ordered, for instance, "no throwing or running with the round ball, but it could be batted or dribbled." The game attracted one hundred New Brunswick fans, who came more out of curiosity than to support any one team or player.

The rival colleges battled to a Rutgers 6–4 victory. Points were scored one at a time by kicking the ball over the goal line, but not through uprights. More games were played, but frustration soon settled in because of the difficulty associated with the rules. Finally, in 1874, needed changes were made.

Records indicate that the first important American coach was Amos Alonzo Stagg. The excitement of football won Coach Stagg's heart and imagination—he had a true passion for the game and loved to encourage younger players. As a Yale divinity student, he began coaching part-time to help pay his tuition. He coached at Springfield College, Massachusetts, then moved to the University of Chicago. At the age of seventy-one, he became the head coach for the University of the Pacific in Stockton, California.

Some historians credit Stagg with developing the forward pass, the T-formation, the single and double flanker, the huddle, the shift, the man in motion, the quick kick, the short kickoff, and the short punt formation. He helped invent numerous elements of football gear, including uniform numbers, the tackling dummy, the blocking sled, and the padded goalpost.

Coach Stagg died in 1965 at the age of 102, having won 314 games. Only a few coaches would ever win more, including the legendary Paul (Bear) Bryant from the University of Alabama, Eddie Robinson of Grambling, and Joe Paterno of Penn State. One of Stagg's disciples, Glenn (Pop) Warner, won 313 games by emphasizing the importance of concentrated practice.

In the 1920s another progressive coach, John Heisman, for whom the trophy honoring the nation's outstanding college player is named, began marketing football in the same way baseball had been promoted. Coach Heisman expanded football throughout the nation, inspiring rule changes that placed a healthy balance between the offensive and defensive aspects of the game.

It was in the same era that the National Football League was formed to take highly skilled college athletes into the professional arena. Coaches like George Halas and Red Grange inspired franchises to begin in cities like Chicago, Green Bay, Cleveland, Cincinnati, Detroit, and Buffalo. Most games were played on dirt fields without much padding or protection for the players. You had to be extra tough to play in this league—most men played both offense and defense, adding to the possibility of sustaining a serious injury.

Without championship games and with poor stadium seating, the unmatched teams of the NFL didn't draw many fans during the dark days of the depression. Baseball was still king, and this newly developing sport seemed more of a nuisance than something of real spectator value. Even so, as NFL Championship contests evolved and players' salaries increased, so did viewership. With more rule changes, better equipment and training programs, faster and more specialized athletes, and the advent of television, folks were able to see and support their favorite team.

Inspirational players rallied fans to frenzy status. Johnny Unitas, Bart Starr, Paul Hornung, Jim Taylor, Y. A. Tittle, George Blanda, and great defensive units like the Steel Curtain of the Pittsburgh Steelers, the Fearsome Foursome of the Los Angeles Rams, the Purple People Eaters of the Minnesota Vikings, the Doomsday Defense of the Dallas Cowboys, and the New York

Sack Exchange of the Jets became icons for a generation of Americans seeking to escape the rigors of a fast-paced society and the fears associated with the cold war.

With the impending merger of the American Football League (AFL) and the National Football League (NFL), a championship game was scheduled for the two titleholders. This super Sunday became the most watched spectacle in television history. Today hundreds of millions of people around the world watch the two top contenders square off for the honor of being crowned Super Bowl Champion.

After long years of ministry, the highly respected Charles Simeon of Cambridge was on his deathbed. As his friends gathered around him, he smiled, asking them, "Do you know the text that comforts me just now?"

"No," they replied. "Tell us."

"I find infinite consolation in the fact that in the beginning God created the heavens and the earth."

Intimate comfort in an infinite God. The creating power of God not only gives us *dying* comfort but also *daily* comfort.

One night during a particularly full moon, I sat on the back porch a long time, gazing through binoculars at God's "lesser light." I could even detect the rough edges of mountains and jagged peaks, and I considered again the splendor of God in designing the universe with rings and orbs, thus giving us endless opportunities for new beginnings.

The earth, being a sphere, spins on its axis. The sun, being round, provides an orbit for the earth. The result? Every sixty seconds, we have a new minute. Every sixty minutes, we have a new hour. Every twenty-four hours, we have a new day. And every 365 days, we have a new year, a new beginning.

"In the beginning God created the heavens and the earth" (Genesis 1:1). God made everything. Through His awesome power He designed it all. I find it interesting to note that with more and more scientific discoveries, many scientists who formerly believed in large-scale evolution as an explanation for the creation of life now feel that there must have been some divine power that brought about the formation of humankind.

It takes *more* faith to believe that through a set of nearly impossible circumstances life just evolved. People who believe this perhaps also have faith that you could put the parts and pieces of a watch into your pocket and walk down the street five miles to suddenly discover that the watch not only put itself together but also set itself to the perfect time.

John begins his gospel with this same prepositional phrase, *In the beginning* (1:1). The verse goes on to say that the eternal preexistence of the Word (Jesus Christ) existed before the universe began. John tells us that the Word was made flesh in Christ Jesus.

Unlike the evolution of football, God's plan and purpose for humankind does not change. Our God is a God of order and reason, and His desire is to have fellowship with His creation. God takes great delight in knowing that those He has made can freely love and praise Him. He wishes to communicate deeply with His dear children, hoping that their desire is to know Him and to make Him known. Do you love, worship, and know Him? He seeks *you!*

For since the creation of the world God's invisible qualities—his eternal power and divine nature—have been clearly seen, being understood from what has been made, so that men are without excuse.

—*Romans 1:20*

> "**I**'ve compared offensive linemen to the story of
> Paul Revere. After Paul Revere rode through town,
> everybody said what a great job he did. But no one
> ever talked about the horse."

—**Gene Upshaw,** Former Raider Guard

11

The "O" Line

Without much fame or recognition, the offensive line does its job. Despite all the media attention that marquee quarterbacks and running backs receive, without a great offensive line the QB wouldn't have time to complete many passes and the running back wouldn't have the holes to shoot through. A good offensive line can take many years to build and, with injury or trade or free agency, only minutes to fall apart.

In 1998 the Minnesota Vikings set several NFL records, primarily because of their great offensive line. With a 15–1 record the Vikings allowed only twenty-five sacks, fewest in their history. They also recorded 6,264 yards of offense, best in the league. The experience on the front line was vast, including Randall McDaniel's eleven Pro Bowl appearances. Yet in 2001, with the free agent departures of Todd Steussie, McDaniel, and Jeff Christy, and then the untimely death of Korey Stringer, this same team is struggling to put together a good line.

When the Dallas Cowboys won Super Bowl XXX, their big and powerful offensive line set the standard for the league. The average weight of the starting five was a stunning 324 pounds. All-Pro Nate Newton said, "What people don't realize is that we're in shape. In the fourth quarter we've still got our stamina."

In football, blocking is one of the most important skills and also one of the least appreciated. Former Super Bowl Coach of the Oakland Raiders and now television commentator John Madden says, "You can design the best offensive plays in football, but if your blockers don't do their job, those plays are worthless." For this reason Madden and many coaches believe that assembling the right group of powerful players to make up the "O" line is perhaps the most important task in football.

If a team is playing well on offense it's usually because the offensive line is having a good day against the opposing defensive line. Holes open up more quickly for the running backs, and quarterbacks have the necessary time to scope the field and pick out open receivers.

However, it's rare to hear much about the offensive line unless someone misses a block or lets his man sack the QB. Unlike the more high profile defensive linemen that usually have nicknames, offensive linemen are normally quiet warriors of the game. Statistics indicate that these humble but powerful giants are usually the brightest men on the field; most finished college with good grades. They often take on a leadership role with the team while becoming mentors to the younger players.

One of the NFL's best offensive linemen was Steve Wisniewski of the Oakland Raiders, a quick and agile 6'4", 290-pound, fourteen-year veteran. Former Raider Coach Jon Gruden had the utmost respect for this guy: "Everyone knows what a great leader Wiz is and how much he contributes to the team. I love him. He is dependable, powerful, consistent, and a real team player."

Today many coaches are drafting more men in the mold of Wiz. They want great strength, height, and stamina compacted in a powerful body that doesn't weigh much over 300 pounds. With the speed of today's players and the increased emphasis upon the "West Coast Offense," more power and speed is needed over the bulk frame seen in many of the huge linemen of the 1980s and 1990s.

When studying the character of God, we find that there are illustrations of His power all around us. Evidence is seen through creation, through changing circumstances, through miracles, and through changed lives.

Relying on God's power gives us confidence, strength, assurance, direction, and boldness to live the Christian life as He intended. Whatever trouble we have on earth, we need to remember that we have an awesome God who is capable of handling our problems. God "is able to do exceeding abundantly beyond all that we ask or think, according to the power that works within us" (Ephesians 3:20 NASB).

During the tough times God wants us to keep focused on the big picture. Remember, our eternal hope rests on the power of God, the power that saved us and will "raise [us] up on the last day" (John 6:40 NASB). That should be the great hope of all Christians—especially those who are enduring major struggles. Praise God that our heavenly destiny is secure, infinitely more secure than anything on earth. Let's look at a few ways God's power can bless us.

- *God Is Our Everything.* King David, in one of his psalms of praise, stated it this way: "Wealth and honor come from you; you are the ruler of all things. In your hands are strength and power to exalt and give strength to all" (1 Chronicles 29:12).
- *God Is Our Rescuer.* He wants us to persevere and continue the fight to the finish. God rescues us with His strength and power if we have asked the Holy Spirit to take control of our lives, "so that your faith might not rest on men's wisdom, but on God's power" (1 Corinthians 2:5).
- *God Is Our Shield.* Even our faith in God is empowered by Him. A Christian's continued faith is evidence of God's protection: "[Believers] through faith are shielded by God's power until the coming of the salvation that is ready to be revealed in the last time" (1 Peter 1:5).
- *God Is Our Deliverer.* It is when we believe that we can trust—the two are synonymous. "For to be sure, he was crucified in weakness, yet he lives by God's power. Likewise, we are weak in him, yet by God's power we will live with him to serve you" (2 Corinthians 13:4).
- *God Wishes to Be Known.* Our challenging ordeals and battles help build character and teach us reliance upon Him. "Yet he saved them for His name's sake, to make His mighty power known" (Psalm 106:8).

Are you relying upon God's power or your own strength? He can direct, equip, and guide you in each decision and action. And like a great lineman,

God will quickly open up holes of opportunity for you to glide through on your way to success.

Yet those who wait for the Lord will gain new strength. . . . They will run and not get tired, they will walk and not become weary.

—*Isaiah 40:31* NASB

"If it was, Army and Navy would be playing for the national championship every year."

—Bobby Bowden, Florida State Coach, when asked if discipline is the key to winning

12

Character Is Everything

As is my custom, I try to watch at least thirty minutes of ESPN each day in order to catch up on all the happenings. A while back I observed a conversation between Keyshawn Johnson and an ESPN reporter. Keyshawn had just signed a multiyear contract making him the highest-paid wide receiver in the NFL. It was notable that the reporter seemed more interested in talking to Keyshawn about his character than his new fortune, and his response served as a reminder to all those in prominent positions: "It is critical for all who have been blessed of God with talent, wisdom, fame, and fortune to remember that we *are* role models."

In *The Message,* Eugene Peterson's paraphrase of the New Testament, he elaborates on the apostle Paul's words to Timothy:

> Concentrate on doing your best for God, work you won't be ashamed of, laying out the truth plain and simple. Stay clear of pious talk that is only talk. Words are not mere words, you know. If they are not backed by a godly life, they accumulate as poison in the soul. (2 Timothy 2:15)

It's about integrity, my friend. As someone once said, "Sow a thought, and you reap an act; sow an act, and you reap a habit; sow a habit, and you reap a character; sow a character, and you reap a destiny."

Chuck Swindoll reminds us, "And so it remains, our character is more important than our position; more important than our fame; more important than any glory; more important than our power, and more vital to our country and families than ever before."

Character and integrity are interchangeable; they mean "doing right on purpose." As the psalmist put it, "Let the Lord judge the peoples. Judge me, O Lord, according to my righteousness, according to my integrity, O Most High" (Psalm 7:8).

The highest reward for a man's toil is not what he gets for it, but rather what he becomes by it.

—*American Way*

"He was a franchise player without a franchise."

—Hank Stram, Sportscaster,
on Archie Manning

13

Teamwork

As the fresh fragrance of the evening dew settles upon the river shoreline outside my window, I'm reminded that autumn is not far off. The surrounding forest with its majestic deciduous trees becomes an easel for God to display His artistic craftsmanship by painting an array of fall colors throughout the landscape.

This is also a time when avid fans are getting ready for some serious FOOTBALL! While teams are finalizing their preseason workouts and trimming their rosters, millions of viewers prepare their living rooms and dens for the weekly boob-tube spectacle.

For an armchair quarterback, there is usually a ritual associated with preparing for the season. A fresh start is important. The fishing equipment is stored until next spring, the "honey-do list" gets caught up, clutter from under the easy chair is vacuumed away, fresh batteries are placed in the remote control, and a new popcorn machine is purchased.

Often Dad will enlist the help of his kids to get the yard in order for the long winter so that routine chores are limited to conserve more time to watch football. Of course these duties are accomplished a great deal quicker when everyone pitches in. We remind our kids that working diligently together we can accomplish much. We call this togetherness TEAM-WORK.

Even the casual observer of the game will probably hear more talk about teamwork than any other topic. The most successful families and teams are the ones whose participants understand how to effectively work together in accomplishing their goals.

Starting with the first mini-camp and leading to the pep talk by the head coach before every game, players will hear about the importance of working together—being on the same page. Having an unselfish heart and being an encouragement to others is something that is difficult to coach. Pride, jealousy, envy, and strife are part of man's fallen nature.

If the linemen don't sacrificially give of their bodies to block their assigned player, even All-Pro running backs have little chance of gaining yardage. *Webster's Dictionary* defines teamwork as "joint action by a group of people, in which individual interests are subordinated to group unity and efficiency; coordinated effort, as of an athletic team."

Such was the case with Paul's agricultural illustration in 1 Corinthians 3. Paul (the one planting) and his faithful partner in ministry, Apollos (the one watering), had their God-appointed work. As an evangelist it was essential for Paul to plant the seeds of hope, love, peace, joy, and salvation among those he contacted. He needed the further teaching and encouragement of someone like Apollos to begin "watering" the seeds of knowledge so people would grow in their faith and obedience to Christ Jesus.

Paul reminds us, "Now to each one the manifestation of the Spirit is given for the common good. . . . All these are the work of one and the same Spirit, and he gives them to each one, just as he determines" (1 Corinthians 12:7, 11).

Committed believers who are obedient to God's leading recognize that we are all part of one team—God's. We work together as sowers, planters, waterers, and harvesters to encourage people to consider the claims of Jesus.

Scripture reminds us that none should look upon their kingdom work with pride or conceit. God calls us to be humble of heart, sacrificing for the good of others. Jesus was the ultimate example of this (Philippians 2:5–8), and the supreme demonstration of humility is when we imitate Him: "We know love by this, that He laid down His life for us; and we ought to lay down our lives for the brethren" (1 John 3:16 NASB).

Let's remember that it's not about being important but doing what is important. Just as with Paul and Apollos, if we don't worry about who gets the credit we will participate in many team victories.

He who plants and he who waters are one; but each will receive his own reward according to his own labor. For we are God's fellow workers.

—*1 Corinthians 3:8–9*

> **"I** said, 'Son, I don't understand it with you. Is it ignorance or apathy?' He said, 'Coach, I don't know and I don't care.'"
>
> —**Frank Layden,** on a former player

14

Spectators or Participants?

I really enjoy watching a good game of football. There's something about the strategy and the teamwork that generates a great deal of excitement. I particularly enjoy watching the decision makers—the coaches. They are filled with so much energy while being driven by their passions to excel. They don't sit back and wait for things to happen. A good coach fully participates in the process of assisting others to do their very best.

Despite disappointment, they persevere! A great coach must have the ability to set aside temporary criticism so that he can focus upon the ultimate goal of the team. Even in defeat these visionaries see opportunities to help build character in themselves and their players. Anyone can be positive and display good character when a team is winning. But it takes a man of real faith and confidence to stay focused and committed when trials prevail. Being a participant requires strength of character.

I really miss the relaxed, easygoing personality of retired New Orleans Saints coach Bum Phillips. He had a way of putting things into perspective. During the very difficult 1985 season, the Saints had lost several close games, as well as three members of the offensive line. They were scheduled to play the vaunted San Francisco 49ers, and Bum's job was on the line. When a reporter asked him, "Do you feel any added pressure to win this season?" Bum responded, "No more pressure than before. All they can do is fire me. They can't kill me or eat me."

Most training camps start off with eighty to eighty-five men. By the time they reach their first regular season game, they will have to trim their rosters to fifty-three. Even with the full contingent of players, only eleven can take the field at once. That means at any given time there are forty-two men who are spectators—not participants.

One of the most challenging jobs of the various position coaches is to keep the players who are not on the field focused on the action immediately at hand. If a player can be a vigilant observer and student of the game he can better prepare himself once his number is called. A good coach knows his players' strengths and weaknesses and will play the best man for the job at any given time. When the coaches can properly coordinate the talents and gifts of their team, they usually see immediate rewards.

In like manner, the Christian life is fully experienced when each of us takes to the field of life using our gifts, talents, interests, and hobbies to the glory of our Lord. Like a good coach, a good pastor will properly assess his congregation and utilize people where they are gifted. An effective Christian is one who knows his/her gifts and seeks the wise counsel of God on how to use them for kingdom work.

The purest form of expression of any gift is when it is expressed with a heart of love and sacrifice toward another person. We should periodically ask ourselves, "Am I using my gifts to honor and glorify God and to uplift other followers?"

Much like a good football team, a church works best when the people work together (participate) for a common good. Someone once said, "A Christian's service involves each person of the Trinity." Spiritual gifts are the sovereign choice of the Holy Spirit; the Son of God chooses the place of our service; and the Father determines the actual working of our ministry. This is made clear for us in 1 Corinthians 12:5–7: "There are different kinds of service, but the same Lord. There are different kinds of working, but the same God works all of them in all men. Now to each one the manifestation of the Spirit is given for the common good."

It's easy to be a spectator. Every Sunday there are millions of fans that sit back and enjoy watching others participate, both in sports and in the ministry of the church. I regularly engage pastors in conversation about the reality that only 10 percent of the congregation does 90 percent of the work—and sometimes 90 percent of the giving as well.

We will be effective as the church of God when each person gets in the game. If we are to make an impact for good, everyone must become involved. I'm reminded of the little boy who volunteered his lunch to Jesus. He was using his gift (John 6:1–14); Jesus took his offering and multiplied it for everyone's benefit. We can all learn something from this young servant's heart.

- God uses what you have to fill a need you never could have filled.
- God uses you where you are to take you where you never could have gone.
- God uses what you can do to accomplish what you never could have done.
- God uses who you are to let you become who you never could have been.

How can God use you today? Are you studying, observing, and preparing for the time He calls your number?

There are different kinds of gifts, but the same Spirit. There are different kinds of service, but the same Lord. There are different kinds of working, but the same God works all of them in all men.

—1 Corinthians 12:4–6

"**H**umility is only seven days away."

—**Barry Switzer,** Former Oklahoma and Cowboys Coach

15

Humble Thyself

Wise words from the New Testament remind us of the importance humility can play in our lives: "Humble yourselves in the presence of the Lord, and He will exalt you" (James 4:10 NASB).

After an exciting touchdown run, it is refreshing to see so many professional football players kneel to the ground to celebrate their success with a quiet, reflective moment. It's a real contrast to the vibrant, ego-centered rampage we saw during most of the 1990s.

Backslapping, head-pounding, and high strutting has its place and reward, but blessed are those who acknowledge the success they've achieved without making a mockery of the game. Excessive celebrations often bring unnecessarily delay and incur deep resentment and bitter criticism from the opposing team. Finally, in 1998, the league said enough is enough! Let's put the emphasis where it belongs—on good sportsmanship and grateful hearts—instead of on those few players wishing to show off their latest dance moves.

When I reflect upon who God is—how He is so powerful, infinitely holy, sovereign, mighty, majestic, glorious—all I can see is my own sin and how ordinary I am. I'm reminded of the humility Isaiah experienced when confronted with the reality of God Almighty. He ended up cursing himself: "Woe is me, for I am ruined (damned)! Because I am a man of unclean lips, and I live among a people of unclean lips; for my eyes have seen the King, the Lord of hosts" (Isaiah 6:5).

In the New Testament we know the disciples were humbled after Jesus stilled the storm on the Sea of Galilee: "They became very much afraid and said to one another, 'Who then is this, that even the wind and the sea obey Him?' " (Mark 4:41 NASB). If we're humbled before the true God, we'll have the same response as these Bible characters.

When people face the holy presence of God in their lives, the natural response is to become fearful. But God does not leave us cowering in terror. Scripture tells us that if we are *humbled in spirit*, knowing that we are *saved by grace*, we will be sanctified (set apart—freed) and ultimately glorified.

The apostle Paul summarizes this in Ephesians 2:4–7 (NASB):

> But God, being rich in mercy, because of His great love with which He loved us, even when we were dead in our transgressions, made us alive together with Christ (by grace you have been saved), and raised us up with Him, and seated us with Him in the heavenly places, in Christ Jesus, in order that in the ages to come He might show the surpassing riches of His grace in kindness toward us in Christ Jesus.

Dear friend, while respecting the power and might of God, remember His great love and gracious heart. The first step to humility is understanding our sinfulness and asking for forgiveness. Christ showed us humility by becoming a man and living as a servant. Let's humbly serve others, then, in a Christlike manner. Next time an athlete takes a moment to give some quiet reflection to God for His goodness, let's give that person an extra hand.

It is when we forget ourselves that we do things that are most likely to be remembered.

—Anonymous

"My parents sent me to Harvard to become a specialist. I don't think they were thinking of this."

—**Pat McInally,** Former Bengal Punter

16

The Kicking Game

I remember watching the longest game in NFL history on Christmas Day 1971. It ran for 82 minutes and 40 seconds (of game time) before it finally ended with a Garo Yepremian field goal that allowed the Dolphins to win, 27–24. I couldn't help but think about the pressure Garo must have felt at that precise moment.

With all the missed opportunities in the game, no one was taking this kick for granted. Whether it's punting or placekicking, a player can quickly become the hero or the scapegoat, depending on where the ball hits his foot. It is mastering that particular contact that allows a player to extend his time in the NFL.

Nothing frustrates most coaches more than a kicker who is unpredictable and erratic in his ability to simply kick the pigskin through the uprights. Kickers are a unique breed. Much of what they do is more mental than physical. It is exactly this issue that causes frustration in the head coach.

He watches the kicker make fifty- and sixty-yard field goals in practice. He reminds his special teams coach to make sure the kicker warms up and has plenty of time kicking into the net on the sidelines before he enters the game. Finally, the coach shouts words of encouragement to the specialist as he runs onto the field. A positive approach to kicking is as important as physical abilities. If he thinks he'll miss, most likely he will.

There probably will never be a kicker as great as my friend Gary Anderson. I first met Gary at a Pro Athletes Outreach program. After playing several years for the Pittsburgh Steelers and the Philadelphia Eagles, he became a free agent and went to the San Francisco 49ers. It was during a chapel program I was doing for the Niners that Gary and I realized we shared the same passion for fishing and hunting.

During a subsequent bass fishing trip in the California Delta, I came to really know the heart and passion of this remarkable man of God. Gary's dad, a former pro soccer player who is a pastor/evangelist in Africa, inspired Gary through Bible stories and coaching. With his support Gary developed into a great high school soccer player.

"My folks were missionaries in Durban, South Africa," says Gary. "I played a great deal of soccer there but never even saw a football field until I came 'across the pond' and attended Syracuse University."

Gary was a walk-on who tried out for the football and rugby teams. He didn't even know the fundamental rules of American football, but he impressed the coaches with his kicking style. After playing four years of college ball and earning All-American honors as a senior, he tried out with the Eagles and Bills. Gary finally signed with the Steelers just before the season began. He's gone on to play more than twenty years of NFL football while becoming a four-time Pro Bowl selection.

No player in the history of the game has scored more points (2,133 and counting). Only one field goal kicker has ever had a perfect season—thirty-five attempts and thirty-five field goals plus fifty-nine PAT (point after touchdown) attempts with fifty-nine successful kicks—and that is Gary Anderson. This was accomplished in 1998 as he was celebrating his thirty-ninth birthday.

The greats like Cleveland's Lou Groza, San Francisco's Gordy Soltau, Washington's Mark Moseley, Kansas City's Jan Stenerud, New Orleans' Morten Andersen, and Oakland's George Blanda—none have as many points as this well-conditioned athlete. Gary's 5'11" frame doesn't do justice to the competitive spirit and the unique character of this outdoorsman.

I remember chatting with him after the 1997 season when the 49ers decided that he probably couldn't kick another year. Gary said, "As long as I feel I can contribute to the game and the good Lord lets me kick—I'm going to kick." It was the next season that he was perfect and selected to go to the Pro Bowl.

One of the reasons for his great success is that Gary never takes for granted the unique gift and abilities God has given him. He works hard at perfecting his trade and never takes even an extra-point try for granted. His abiding faith and his inspirational approach to the game have helped encourage many younger players and even this old sage. I regret that because of his leaving the Bay Area, I only had a little over a year to know and be inspired by Gary.

In case you worry that you've missed the best, keep an eye on another great kicker and mature believer, Kansas City's Todd Peterson. He already enjoys a great deal of success with three consecutive 100-point seasons and the highest field goal accuracy in the league (80.7 percent). Todd is a great leader and has a willing heart to share his faith.

Placekickers are especially careful in choosing a holder with good hands and a calm spirit. The holder is to the kicker what a reel is to a fishing rod; they must work in perfect harmony in order to complete the job. A holder is usually one of the kicker's best and most trusted friends.

After taking the snap, a holder must spin the ball so the laces face the goalpost. If the laces are anywhere but straight forward the ball can wobble, reduce in distance, or lose accuracy. The ball is centered exactly to the kicker's preference so that each kick will be placed in the same position relative to the holder's hands.

Confidence in the holder is key to the success of every kick. The kicker must be totally confident that the holder will do everything in his power to place the ball in the correct spot at the precise time his foot hits the ball. Lou Groza once said, "Never worry about missing a field goal. Just blame the holder and think about kicking the next one."

Many special teams work extra hard to intimidate the kicker. They realize that if they can get into his head and make him feel that they can block the ball, the kicker will rush and perhaps cause the ball to fly low or askew. So it is in life. There are times others can get into our heads and cause us to miss a blessing or to succumb to a temptation. Being surrounded by inspirational friends like Gary Anderson—friends who are centered on God's Word and who can provide godly wisdom and counsel—can encourage us to stay on the right track.

The book of Proverbs is full of great advice about the benefits of having a good friend, a buddy you can count on. We all need someone to hold those unique burdens, placing them into proper prospective so we can kick them

where they belong—into the hands of a caring and loving God.
Do you have such a friend? Are *you* such a friend?

A friend loves at all times, and a brother is born for adversity.
—*Proverbs 17:17*

"He faked me out so bad one time I got a fifteen-
yard penalty for grabbing my own facemask."

—D. D. Lewis, Former Cowboy Linebacker,
on Franco Harris

17

Fakes

I grew up in an area of East Oakland where most of the kids in my neighborhood could run fast. I was very gangly, with legs like stilts, so speed was something I could only dream about. I didn't have the flat-out quickness of my friends, but I learned to compensate. Early in my limited football experience as a receiver I realized that there was more than one way to get open. Deception and trickery often worked. My fakes and jukes would create separation between the speedy coverage men and me. This would allow me to make strategic catches.

It's no secret why players like Hall-of-Famer Fred Biletnikoff of the Oakland Raiders and Ed McCaffrey of the Denver Broncos have been so successful. They've not only used a tremendous work ethic, great hands, precise patterns, and a desire to perfect their position, but both men are unbelievably deceptive. While not as fast as most receivers, they've used deception (fakes) to fool the cornerbacks assigned to cover them.

A fake could be as simple as a head bob in one direction, a short cut in the opposite direction they intend to go, or pretending to catch a throw that hasn't even been made. Anything that will throw off the pace and speed of the defender will aid the receiver in getting separation.

Biletnikoff played fourteen seasons for the Raiders before becoming a coach. Today Ed McCaffrey continues to amaze fans with acrobatic catches and amazing stamina. While deceptions work well for a receiver, in the Word of God we are cautioned to be on the lookout for "fakes."

We are constantly being fooled by fakes of one kind or another. Unless you live in a box you will face those who are charlatans and deceivers. They are quick to win your trust and confidence only to take advantage of your gracious generosity or kindness.

Many folks seeking to find hope and assurance buy into the advertisements in the hope of finding encouragement from an assortment of psychics, astrologers, and soothsayers who do not rely on Christ as their Lord. The Bible warns us against these "false prophets" who are demon-driven and full of trickery.

We are cautioned not to fall into the trap of thinking that the teaching of these false prophets is harmless. Many Hollywood personalities and some very visible NFL players who endorse things like crystals, tarot cards, palm reading, or other such trickery find it reassuring to share their "readings" with an audience. But Scripture is clear about believing in such things or even spending time with these cultic tools: "Do not be carried away by all kinds of strange teachings" (Hebrews 13:9).

The above practices are not harmless. They have the potential to creep into our thoughts and attitudes. These "fakes" and their messed-up teachings can direct our resources and attention onto things that ultimately lead to evil. Even some "religious leaders" are not exempt. They take Scripture out of context and lead their innocent followers into believing that they have mystical powers. Leaders like Guyana's Jim Jones or Waco's David Koresh are examples of how cults can capture the heart, imagination, hope, and finances of unsuspecting individuals.

In Rita McKenzie Fisher's book titled *Lessons From the Gridiron*, she describes some ways we can test a person to be sure we are not being "faked out":

> Do they merely use the name of Jesus or do they truly honor Him? Is salvation only through Christ or by their own divine nature? Do they add "new revelations" from God or do they rely on His Word as written? Are they open and honest or exclusive and secretive? Is their loyalty to Jesus or to the group leader? Do they publicize financial statements or keep records secret? Are the leader's views the only ones accepted or can you read the Bible and pray out loud by yourself?

If you receive incorrect answers to these questions, beware! Watch out for "fakes"—they will put you out of position to catch the truth.

I am sending you out like sheep among wolves.
Therefore be as shrewd as snakes and as innocent as doves.
—*Matthew 10:16*

"I want to win a championship.... It's probably what I want right now more than anything else in the world. But if I don't, I'm not going to kill myself. And if I do win a championship, it will probably make me happier than anything else could—right now. But in a few years, it won't make much difference."

—Fran Tarkenton

Chapter

First Quarter

Confidence is contagious. So is lack of confidence.

—Vince Lombardi

"**G**eorge Halas was famous for being associated with only one club all his life—the one he held over your head during salary talks."

—Bobby Layne

18

Being a Competent Leader

Leadership is the power to evoke the proper response from others in order to obtain a selected goal. People who have good leadership skills are usually those who have been tested and tried under stressful situations. Walter Lippmann said, "The final test of a leader is that he leaves behind him in other men the conviction and the will to carry on."

The fall and winter are times when every weekend and Monday night we see outstanding examples of young men displaying leadership skills that can help encourage and motivate their football teams to victory. We call these warriors of the gridiron "quarterbacks."

When surveying players and coaches as to what makes a good team leader, words like *dedication, commitment, passion, perseverance, determination,* and *mental toughness* come up. As we closely observe marquee players and see the way others look up to them, we are impressed that they model these qualities in every aspect of their lives. These traits become second nature to them.

The last regular season game of 2000–2001 featured "The Battle of the Bay," where two of my favorite teams clashed in one of the best NFL match-ups of the year. The 49ers' quarterback, Jeff Garcia, and the Raiders' leader, Rich Gannon, provided viewers with some exciting lessons on leadership. The dynamics and interaction between the players and coaches of both these great teams is exciting to see. The demonstration of professional leadership skills from the quarterbacks is textbook MBA stuff.

Over the past ten years I've observed many talented coaches and players. It's interesting to see vibrant leadership traits emerge during stressful situations. Let's look at just a few of the qualities good leaders possess:

- Most successful and influential men are quick to encourage others.
- They recognize the value and importance of promoting and utilizing the gifts of others to accomplish a goal.
- Leaders like to direct people to a positive future and vision.
- An influential person will motivate people to achieve their very best.
- He will strive to maintain unity and harmony among his teammates.
- A naturally gifted person will take charge and obtain respect due to his modeling of a proper attitude and exemplary behavior.
- A great leader sacrifices for others so that their common vision might be reached.

I'm reminded of a story about certain sailors in ancient times that displayed unbelievable leadership. During the time of Christ the strongest swimmers among a ship's crew were called *archegos*, a Greek word that means "front-runner" or "pioneer." When a ship approached an unstable shoreline, where a safe beach landing was not assured, captains would call upon the *archegos* to jump into the pounding surf and swim ashore with a rope fastened to his waist. Once ashore he would fasten the long rope from the boat to the landing, usually seeking out a large rock or significant tree to quickly secure the line. Then the other passengers and crew could disembark and use the rope as a safety tether to reach the shore.

As Christians, Jesus is our *archegos*. Without His sacrificial death and resurrection we would be lost—our individual Christian lives would be a frustrating exercise in futility. As the apostle Paul stated, "If we have hoped in Christ in this life only [meaning, if Christ has not been resurrected], we are of all men most to be pitied" (1 Corinthians 15:19 NASB). But Jesus left us with a brighter hope: "For the wages of sin is death, but the gift of God is eternal life in Christ Jesus our Lord" (Romans 6:23 NASB).

Likewise, if all there is to life is the next NFL game, we above all men are to be pitied. Pray for the ability to develop the leadership skills of an *archegos*. Focus on developing Christlike leadership skills that will help mold and shape your character and inspire your family.

When a man is able to take abuse with a smile, he is worthy to become a leader.

—*Nachman of Bratslav*

> "We didn't coach him, we just aimed him."

> —**Gary Phillips,** Herschel Walker's high school coach

19

Mind Over Matter

The mind is a powerful thing and greatly influences our behavior for good or for evil. The legendary Alabama coach, Paul ("Bear") Bryant, told of a unique moment in 'Bama history when, with two minutes remaining in a critical game against their rival, a miracle of the mind happened.

Alabama was first and ten on the opponent's twenty-yard line. They had a five-point lead with no timeouts remaining for either team. Bryant's starting quarterback took the ball on a quarterback sneak and was hit hard—his pain was such that he had to remove himself from the game. Coach Bryant found his rookie backup quarterback and told him the following: "This game is ours if you do what I say. I want you to rush the ball all three remaining downs. Do *not*, under any circumstance, put it up in the air. Even if we don't make a first down, there will be so little time left on the clock that our defense will hold them until the game is over." The coach focused his gaze and said, "Do you understand?" With a big gulp the young man responded, "Yes sir, I understand: Don't put the ball in the air."

The rookie ran onto the field and immediately called an off-tackle play that gained no yards. On the third down he executed a sneak and gained one yard. On the last down, with just seconds remaining in the game, the nervous quarterback once again called an off-tackle play. This time the running back missed the handoff, leaving the ball in the quarterback's hands. The frightened rookie looked up to see his tight end frantically waving his arms in the end zone. He was wide open. The quarterback knew that all he had to do was lob a pass and the game was over.

What he didn't know was that an All-American safety had let the tight end roam free, hoping the quarterback would throw in that direction. The safety had lightning-quick speed and planned to intercept the ball.

As the pass was released, the safety moved toward it with the speed and grace of a cheetah. The talented defensive back grabbed the spiraling ball and began his journey, 100 yards to 'Bama's end zone.

The rookie quarterback was the only person who had a chance to tackle the elusive defender. He chased the safety down the field and finally tackled him on his own two-yard line just as the whistle blew ending the game.

As the game ended, the two coaches met in the center of the field to exchange handshakes. The perplexed coach of the opposing team asked Coach Bryant, "According to our scouting reports, your rookie quarterback isn't very swift on his feet. How on earth did he catch our guy—one of the quickest in college football?"

With that famous southern accent, Coach Bryant drawled, "Your man was running for six points. My boy was running for his life!"

Yes, our minds affect our actions. We can have the best intentions to do what is right, but if our mind is undisciplined we can be tempted to do evil. God's Word tells us to be *single-minded* in purpose and intent. We are to focus our thoughts on things that are pure, truthful, admirable, noble, and of good character. If our minds are disciplined we will be less likely to give way to temptation or to worry. With a disciplined mind we will enjoy a more peaceful life.

The apostle Paul says,

> Do not be anxious about anything, but in everything, by prayer and petition, with thanksgiving, present your requests to God. And the *peace* of God, which transcends all understanding, will guard your hearts and your *minds* in Christ Jesus. Finally, brothers, whatever is true, whatever is noble, whatever is right, whatever is pure, whatever is lovely, whatever is admirable—if anything is excellent or praiseworthy—think about such things. (Philippians 4:4–8, emphasis added)

The "*stronghold* factor" reveals that the mind can't focus on two things at once. If our attention is on those things that bring honor to God and to our family, we will be less likely to have fear, worry, and temptation rule our actions. Remember: We are fighting a spiritual battle. "What causes fights and quarrels among you? Don't they come from your desires that battle within you?" (James 4:1). Paul reminds us that we need to develop a stronghold of faith and of thought to conquer temptation: "For our struggle is not against flesh and blood, but against the rulers, against the authorities, against the powers of this dark world and against the spiritual forces of evil in the heavenly realms" (Ephesians 6:12).

Finally, we are to *surrender* to God. His Word tells us to choose our thoughts. By surrendering our desires and our will, the Holy Spirit will help guide our attitudes and actions. We are to dethrone the devil in our lives and enthrone Christ. Only the power of God can help us overcome the daily temptations life brings:

> Though we live in the world, we do not wage war as the world does. The weapons we fight with are not the weapons of the world. On the contrary, they have divine power to demolish strongholds. We demolish arguments and every pretension that sets itself up against the knowledge of God, and we take captive every thought to make it obedient to Christ. (2 Corinthians 10:3–5)

Holiness is not the way to Christ; Christ is the way to holiness. God does not change you to love you; God loves you in order that He may change you. He communicates with us through our minds. If you truly wish to change the way you live, you need to change the way you think.

◄■►

You were taught, with regard to your former way of life, to put off your old self, which is being corrupted by its deceitful desires; to be made new in the attitude of your minds.

—Ephesians 4:22–23

> "**W**aiting for the Rams to win a Super Bowl is like leaving the porch light on for Jimmy Hoffa."
>
> —**Milton Berle**, Comedian

20

From Supermarket to Super Bowl

It has been called the "Greatest Single-Season Sports Story in History!" Kurt Warner's long road to gridiron success was filled with setbacks and bad breaks. He warmed the bench for four years at the University of Northern Iowa. Finally getting a chance as a fifth-year senior, he led the Panthers to the NCAA Division 1-AA semifinals and was named the Gateway Conference Offensive Player of the Year. But he was passed over in the NFL draft and rejected by the Canadian Football League. When all else failed, Warner took a job stocking shelves for $5.50 an hour at the Hy-Vee Supermarket in Cedar Falls, Iowa, while he worked out at a college practice field during his time off.

A year later he was playing again, but in small-time Arena League football, an indoor game using eight players on a side and fifty-yard fields. He missed a tryout for the Chicago Bears in 1997 when he was bitten on the elbow by a venomous spider, leaving him unable to throw.

After three years he took a step up. He was signed by the Rams and was sent to the Amsterdam Admirals of NFL Europe, where in the spring of 1998 he led the league in passing yardage and touchdowns.

The Rams put him on the team for the 1998–1999 season, but he played in only one game. He was left unprotected in the expansion draft, but the new Cleveland Browns didn't want him. Warner was still with the Rams in early 1999 at minimum pay, but they didn't appreciate his full potential and signed QB Trent Green before the season for $16.5 million. It looked like Warner would be riding the bench again as a backup.

But Green got hurt, and it opened the door for Warner to show his stuff. He capped off a Cinderella season by passing the Rams to victory in Super Bowl XXXIV. He not only won the game and was voted MVP, but he also gained the hearts of many Americans.

By the end of the playoffs, much to the surprise of almost everyone, he had thrown a record 49 touchdown passes, led the league in completion percentage, and taken the Rams to the best record in the NFC: 13–3. His 109.2 quarterback rating put him in the same class as his idols, Joe Montana and Steve Young. In five months he had gone from anonymity to being a Pro Bowler and an MVP.

Through it all Warner remembered his faith, his family, and his friends. He believes it is important to "keep first things first." His great humility was underscored when he stood before a Billy Graham Crusade audience of more than forty thousand and said, "Whether I'm a Super Bowl Champion or a regular guy stocking groceries at the Hy-Vee, sharing my faith and glorifying Jesus is the central focus of my time on this earth. . . . I want to be a role model for Christ in everything I do."

In a time when so many players are looking for every opportunity to beat their own drum, it is refreshing to see a man as humble as Kurt Warner. He and his lovely wife, Brenda, continually work with their three kids on developing great character.

I'm reminded of numerous verses in Scripture that help me appreciate that whatever our gifts and talents are, whatever we're able to do from a physical, mental, or spiritual standpoint, or whatever our perceived successes, *we owe it all to God.* Moses reminded the Israelites before they entered the Promised Land: "You may say in your heart, 'My power and the strength of my hand made me this wealth.' But you shall remember the Lord your God, for it is He who is giving you power to make wealth" (Deuteronomy 8:17–18 NASB).

The Warners realize that everything we have, everything we are, is because of God's grace and strength in our lives. It is good to remember that

Satan will tempt us to be prideful and haughty in spirit because of our abilities and accomplishments, but we must realize that every good thing we have is from the Lord. Paul asks us, "What do you have that you did not receive?" (1 Corinthians 4:7 NASB).

I believe God wants us to have a "healthy pride" in what we do but not be prideful. He wants us to do our very best in everything. The Lord desires that we work hard in our jobs, develop relationships, and encourage our families in serving Him. He has shown us by example that it is good to be joyful after we have accomplished something wonderful. In Genesis we see God affirming himself after each creation by saying, "It is good." And when He finished creating man and woman He said, "It is *very* good."

Having a healthy pride in our efforts demonstrates proper respect for self and for our Creator. God was demonstrating self-respect, self-satisfaction, self-sufficiency, self-content, and self-confidence when He affirmed himself. He desires that we enjoy feelings of satisfaction and contentment from a job well done. Warner's locker room talk after the Super Bowl demonstrated the proper balance of self-respect and faith.

God's Word speaks against a prideful spirit and a heart that testifies to vanity, conceit, egoism, narcissism, self-love, and self-glorification. Pride, like many other things, is a two-edged sword. It can be used to glorify God, or it can be used to disgrace and embarrass our heavenly Father, friends, and family.

Kurt Warner and many other Christian athletes realize who has empowered them and who ultimately should receive the credit. Warner's faith in Christ has given him the peace and strength he's needed to handle all the challenges that have come his way. He admits, "Before I could devote my life to Jesus and start living my life for Him, I had to go through a lot of personal struggles, including a period a few years ago where I got caught up in things that aren't important—fame, money, lust. . . ."

I know Warner would agree that the most damaging pride is external spirituality without internal holiness. Jesus reserved His greatest condemnations for those who had such pride:

> Woe to you, scribes and Pharisees, hypocrites! For you are like whitewashed tombs which on the outside appear beautiful, but inside they are full of dead men's bones and all uncleanness. Even so you outwardly appear righteous to men, but inwardly you are full of hypocrisy and lawlessness. (Matthew 23:27–28 NASB)

Let's examine our hearts to make sure our pride is in God and not in our position, possessions, power, intelligence, or spirituality.

A man's pride brings him low, but a man of lowly spirit gains honor.
—Proverbs 29:23

21

Run, Baby, Run

It was a cool fall afternoon in 1994 at the University of Washington football stadium—the beginning of another season. One of the best college running backs of all time was poised to take the field for his last year. The legendary "tunnel" leading to the field was electrified with tension as Napoleon Kaufman and his teammates stood and contemplated the game and their futures. Just two weeks prior to that moment, as a confused young man, Kaufman had been in a street fight after a night of clubbing and drinking. Napoleon recalls, "It was all about me. My world consisted of acting like a fool so that others would recognize me. I was living a life built on external rewards that I thought would make me happy. In my heart, I knew I was living a lie."

Known as Nip to his teammates, he remembers wondering if he could get through that first game. Doctors had worked hours to try to reconstruct his eye socket due to the injury suffered in the street brawl. His physician had advised him to give up football due to the fragile nature of the screws that were placed in his head during surgery.

"That season was difficult, as I was filled with fear and worry," Kaufman says. "I was constantly trying to meet everyone's expectations while feeling that I could fumble at any time. Being one of the smallest players in the game, I often felt threatened."

Kaufman finished the season and over his collegiate career led the Pac-10 with 4,041 rushing yards and set numerous Washington Huskies records. He did so well his name was placed in contention for the coveted Heisman and Doak Walker awards. In the spring of 1995 he was the first-round draft pick of the Oakland Raiders.

Despite his success, inwardly Kaufman knew that his life was a mess. His arrogant attitude and foul mouth baited others to confrontation. He showed disrespect to players by placing his primary focus on his personal accomplishments and scores. But inside he was struggling. His precious new bride beckoned him to be a leader at home. His teammates encouraged him to "quit actin' a fool." Through a series of events both on and off the field he felt that "God was trying to tell him something." People began sending him Christian books; strangers began coming up to him and saying things like, "God has a plan for you. He wants to use your life for kingdom work."

Kaufman knew that in the past pro athletes were known and admired for being *record breakers,* and he realized that many of today's athletes are known for being *lawbreakers.* He didn't want to end up an embarrassment to himself, to his family, or to God. Kaufman recalls a conversation he had with fullback Jerome Davidson that impressed him with the grace and peace that only a life in Christ can bring.

That night Kaufman gave his life to Jesus. Both he and his wife, Nicole, were baptized and motivated to study God's Word. Instead of focusing on himself, he now focuses upon God's plan for his life. Instead of being an embarrassment to the team, he was a role model. Instead of worrying about external rewards, he now places his attention on the internal blessings that come with a dedicated life.

Kaufman now sees trials as a testing ground for his faith. He agrees with James (the half brother of Christ): "Consider it pure joy, my brothers, whenever you face trials of many kinds, because you know that the testing of your faith develops perseverance. Perseverance must finish its work so that you may be mature and complete, not lacking anything" (James 1:2–4).

And, like the psalmist, Kaufman constantly remembers that during the fearful times, "I will fear no evil, for you are with me" (Psalm 23:4).

Kaufman's best season came after he accepted Christ into his heart; in 1997 he rushed for 1,294 yards, which was the all-time second best total for an Oakland Raider. His quickness and superior decision-making skills propelled him to become one of the most outstanding running backs in the NFL. He, Nicole, Nippy, and Nathanael live in Danville, California, and are engaged in an exciting ministry called "Crucified With Christ." His book *At the Cross* is a worthwhile investment.

So I sought for a man among them who would . . .
stand in the gap before Me.

—*Ezekiel 23:30* NKJV

> **"A**ll I know is that we went out there in two buses and came back in one."
>
> —**Gene Stallings,** Former Texas A & M Defensive End, when asked if practice had been tough

22

Perseverance: The Athlete's Friend

In the preseason of 2001 a popular *East Bay* newspaper sports section headline read, "Wisniewski says decision is forthcoming." The columnist went on to describe this remarkable player. "He's the model citizen, the consummate professional, always present and never late." Despite one year remaining on his contract, Steve was leaning in the direction of quitting football to go into ministry full time. When I think of the perseverance needed to be a successful athlete, I'm reminded of my good friend All-Pro Guard Steve Wisniewski, affectionately known as "the Wiz."

Wiz has received almost every honor imaginable for his abilities on the gridiron. He has been asked to appear in eight Pro Bowls and has been recognized by *Sports Illustrated* as one of the toughest guys in football because of his great strength and perseverance. Among his Oakland Raider teammates, Steve is known for his competitive spirit and dynamic power.

After playing the last game of the 1996 season, Wisniewski sat in the locker room and reflected on the difficult year the Raiders had experienced. There were numerous disappointments and lost opportunities that cost them a chance at the playoffs. He decided to commit himself to becoming an even better athlete and a better person.

He decided to prepare himself for a marathon run. The very next day he met with his strength coach and asked for his help: "Coach, I really want to run a complete marathon. This is something I've got to do!" said the bulky-bodied warrior. His huge frame is not exactly suited for a distance runner. In fact, the coaches were not excited about Steve's decision. They were worried that the tedious running could be detrimental to his knees and back, and they felt the constant pavement pounding necessary to prepare for the long-distance event would ultimately take its toll on their valuable player's body. Linemen are not disciplined to do long-distance running but rather to short, powerful bursts of energy.

His first effort at distance was anything but glamorous. He ran a mile and a quarter and collapsed with his lungs burning. "I have never felt so challenged. My big body wasn't made to be tested in that way. I thought I was in good shape until I started jogging for distance," confides the Wiz.

He decided that preparing for a marathon was a good physical and mental discipline to prepare him for life. He had been a Christian since he was a high school athlete but never really challenged himself in his faith and personal commitment to serving God. He decided, "Like the apostle Paul I wanted to live a dedicated and committed life. I wanted to dedicate this marathon to God as a personal sacrifice and testimony of my consecrated life." (See Hebrews 12:1–29.)

He remembered how the perseverance and dedication associated with outdoor sports helped shape his young life. Knowing that an even greater commitment would be required to further mold his relationship with God, he decided that the marathon would serve as a metaphor for the depth of his commitment.

Wiz fixed his gaze on the goal and began a disciplined daily workout that would ultimately lead to participating in the Olympia, Washington, marathon on May 18, 1997. Every day when he hit the track he had one thing in mind: "To honor and glorify God through this testing." Finally, after months of practice, and losing thirty-eight pounds, he lined up with thousands of other runners to begin the 26.2-mile journey to the finish line. Physically, he knew he was in the best condition of his life; the real test would be the mental aspect of the run. He looked to God for strength as he focused on these verses:

> Let us fix our eyes on Jesus, the author and perfecter of our faith, who for the joy set before him endured the cross, scorning its shame, and sat down at the right hand of the throne of God. Consider him who endured

such opposition from sinful men, so that you will not grow weary and lose heart. (Hebrews 12:2–3)

Endure hardship as discipline; God is treating you as sons. For what son is not disciplined by his father? If you are not disciplined (and everyone undergoes discipline), then you are illegitimate children and not true sons. (Hebrews 12:7–8)

Do you not know that in a race all the runners run, but only one gets the prize? Run in such a way as to get the prize. Everyone who competes in the games goes into strict training. They do it to get a crown that will not last; but we do it to get a crown that will last forever. Therefore I do not run like a man running aimlessly; I do not fight like a man beating the air. No, I beat my body and make it my slave so that after I have preached to others, I myself will not be disqualified for the prize. (1 Corinthians 9:24–27)

Wiz knew the odds of a man his size finishing a race this long were very slim. While he had prepared himself well, he felt he needed some additional resources to get through the day:

I decided that I needed some music and some food. I bought a large elastic belt that held my Walkman, extra tapes, and some quick-energy stuff. I hadn't practiced with this equipment and soon realized that the extra weight and bulk of everything really threw me off. It became an encumbrance to performing the way I had practiced.

After about four miles he grasped the meaning of Hebrews 12:1: "Therefore, since we are surrounded by such a great cloud of witnesses, let us throw off everything that hinders and the sin that so easily entangles, and let us run with perseverance the race marked out for us."

He ripped off the belt with all its weight and distractions and threw it into a nearby bush, where he could retrieve it later.

It was five hours and thirty-three minutes from the sound of the starting gun when Steve crossed the finish line. He was the last person to finish and one of very few folks over 270 pounds to ever complete a marathon. What he won was a deeper appreciation for the presence of God in his life. He realized the importance of working hard and persevering toward a goal. He recognized that the difference between ordinary and extraordinary is most often a little extra effort. Scripture encourages us to excel and work hard as unto the Lord.

What goal has God put before you? Are you willing to persevere and sacrifice to get it?

As you know, we consider blessed those who have persevered. You have heard of Job's perseverance and have seen what the Lord finally brought about. The Lord is full of compassion and mercy.

—*James 5:11*

> "**V**ince Lombardi has to have the highest threshold of pain in the world; none of our injuries hurts him at all."
>
> —**Jerry Kramer,** Former Packer Guard

23

Playing Hurt

Football has long been considered the game of life by many philosophically driven personalities. From his experiences with the game as a young athlete, Dr. Larry Wilhite, a management consultant, would attest to that theory.

His first time playing organized football came when he was a freshman in high school. He attended a small school in Idaho that had an enrollment of about one hundred students. There were only about twenty-five boys eligible for varsity football—most with little talent beyond being able to fog a mirror during a physical exam.

Larry was naturally big—as a freshman he weighed 220 pounds and stood over six feet tall. As usual, that summer he bucked hay bales for his uncle and developed muscles where most kids only dreamed of having them. In fact, he had a reputation: They called him the "Human Haying Machine." Fortunately for him, and possibly others, he was clueless about his physical attributes. He was just like any other kid his age—he wanted to look like someone else and he wanted to be someone else. Larry turned out for the varsity and began preseason conditioning. The small contingent of players called it "practice."

Given the brutal nature of the sport and the few players the coach had to choose from, Larry had to be a welcome sight. However, he knew little about football. The only thing this big guy knew was that he had to make the team or suffer great personal disappointment and embarrassment among his friends and family who encouraged him to play.

Practice went on for a week, and Larry loved it—he was a very coachable kid. He hung on every word the coach uttered and made every effort to impress the team with his attitude and enthusiasm. If the coach said jump, Larry asked how high on the way up. In everything the freshman did he doubled his effort in an attempt to be what the coach wanted him to be.

As practice continued, the philosophy of the experience began to sink in. Larry was impressed with what the coaches were telling him: "The first hit of the game is the most important. Hit the other guy harder and more times than he hits you. Do your job better than the other guy 85 percent of the time and you will win!" It made a lot of sense.

As the team was beginning to get the flow of the game, the coach began to talk about the pain and sacrifice required to play football. It seemed to the team that he was developing their courage so that they wouldn't be fearful. Due to the limited number of players, the coach told them, "Be prepared to play hurt." Larry understood the concept. He was confident and anxious to proceed.

Finally it came time to pass out equipment. The poor school district had little or no athletic budget so most of the equipment consisted of hand-me-downs from larger school districts. To make matters worse, the freshmen were the last to get their gear.

Everything about Larry's uniform was wrong. If an item was supposed to fit tight, it fit loose. If an item was to fit loose, it fit tight. His shoulder pads were half the size he needed and the helmet was too big for his head—it wobbled when he ran. Given the nature of the game and the condition of the equipment, it was a good bet that sometime during the season most of the players were going to get hurt.

Game day finally arrived, and the big freshman was quite a sight. If a cartoonist were to sketch him, he would have looked like two humps on a camel with a large bombardier helmet in the middle. But there he was, a starter on the varsity squad, playing both offense and defense. As Larry stepped onto the field his mind began to rush with the coach's challenges:

"Hit first, hit hard, hit often, and be prepared to play hurt."

The game began with a flurry. The first play on offense was called over Larry's tackle position. He sized up the guy across the "trench" and felt confident that he could take him. The ball was snapped, and he fired off from his stance like a cannonball. There was a huge collision, a big pile of humanity stacked up on the thirty-yard line in a cloud of dust, and Larry was somewhere in the middle.

As the pile began to unfold, something was wrong. Larry suddenly realized he must be hurt. The coach's words welled up in him. He managed to get up, but had great difficulty seeing. His left eye was blind, and he had tunnel vision in the right. One of the seniors grabbed the wobbly freshman and got him into the next play. Larry appeared to be injured, but he was playing. Somehow he managed to work his way back to his team's side of the field, and then he heard it. The coach yelled, "WILHITE! TURN YOUR HELMET AROUND. YOU'RE LOOKING THROUGH THE EAR HOLE!"

Larry learned a great deal about football that day, some of it a little embarrassing. He learned an important thing about life, too: Attitude has a lot to do with *how* you do.

Charles Swindoll expresses the importance of having the right attitude:

> The longer I live, the more I realize the impact of attitude on life. Attitude to me is more important than facts. It is more important than the past, than education, than money, than circumstances, than failures, than successes, than what other people think or say or do. It is more important than appearances, giftedness, or skill. It will make or break a company . . . a church . . . a home. The remarkable thing is we have a choice every day regarding the attitude we will embrace for that day. We cannot change our past . . . we cannot change the fact that people will act a certain way. We cannot change the inevitable. The only thing we can do is play on the one string we have, and that is our attitude. . . . I am convinced that life is 10 percent what happens to us and 90 percent how we react to it. And so it is with you . . . we are in charge of our attitudes.

We win with the right attitude, and everyone we touch on any given day wins by how we act and react with them. So on the first play of each day, project your best attitude, sustain it at least 85 percent of the time, and even when you "gotta play hurt," do it with a good attitude. When you do, you win, and everyone else wins too! (Adapted from *The Ultimate Adventure Magazine*, vol. 1, no. 2, 2000, published by LGFM.)

It didn't do any good. My neck still hurts.
—*Ira Gordon, former Buccaneer Guard,*
after an X-ray

> **"W**e'll definitely be improved this year. Last year we lost ten games. This year we only scheduled nine."
>
> —**Ray Jenkins,** former Montana State Coach

24
Confidence

Every January we focus on the critical playoff games. We usually see players performing at their very best as they compete for the coveted prize of the championship. I'm convinced that the confidence of the quarterback is a key factor in the outcome of any team's efforts. When a QB passes the ball, there are basically four possibilities: a completion, an incompletion, a penalty, or an interception. With those odds, a QB needs a great deal of confidence to be successful. If he loses confidence in himself, his offensive line, his coaches, or his receivers, he runs a high risk of failure.

When you think about great quarterbacks you immediately focus upon their swagger or their positive spirit. Tittle, Unitas, Starr, Bradshaw, Namath, Griese, Fouts, Warner, Staubach, Tarkenton, Montana, Young, Aikman, Favre, and Gannon are but a few of the standouts who pop into my mind. It is interesting to analyze these players and their personal makeup. Most of them were/are not big in stature, extremely muscular, or particularly fast, but all of them possessed tremendous leadership skills and a unique self-confidence.

When we look into the significance of the word we find that *confidence* is a firm belief in one's abilities to accomplish a task. It is the fact of being or feeling certain, assured, or reliant upon one's power to succeed.

In his book *Play Football the NFL Way*, Tom Bass states, "Height and weight may vary considerably from one quarterback to another, but all successful quarterbacks have an inner strength and belief in themselves." To be triumphant a quarterback needs to bring an air of confidence onto the field and into the huddle. His motivating spirit becomes contagious and is quickly transmitted. Great quarterbacks exude confidence in their team, their coaches, their play-calling abilities, and their God-given skills.

Confidence can be two-sided. When an affirming spirit becomes conceited or arrogant, it becomes a turnoff to the very people we are trying to motivate. As believers in Christ we need to be confident about our relationship with God while exuding a compassionate, caring spirit to others.

When the apostle Paul was facing the executioner's sword, he did so with an assurance that had sustained him through trying times. His ministry was full of danger, and yet he wouldn't have had it any other way—he was serving his Lord. Paul knew that through his belief and trust in God he would eventually find perfect peace. He had confidence and assurance in his Savior.

Let's approach life with a confident spirit, displaying the same attitude Paul wrote about in Philippians 1:3–6:

> I thank my God every time I remember you. In all my prayers for all of you, I always pray with joy because of your partnership in the gospel from the first day until now, being *confident* of this, that he who began a good work in you will carry it on to completion until the day of Christ Jesus (emphasis added).

I am confident in the Lord.

—*Galatians 5:10*

> "One man practicing sportsmanship is far better than fifty preaching it."
>
> —Knute Rockne

25

Building Character

Some time ago Deion Sanders, a.k.a. "Neon Deion" or "Prime Time," stated, "As a kid I admired many athletes for certain traits they displayed . . . and incorporated them into myself." He liked the brashness and confidence of Muhammad Ali; he also emulated the focus Hank Aaron had during his chase of Babe Ruth's home-run record. Similarly, Prime Time liked the class and respect demonstrated by Julius Erving on and off the basketball court.

However, Sanders is quick to remind us, "These weren't the people who ultimately instilled my morals and taught me right from wrong." He places that responsibility with his parents and on a pastor friend, Bishop T. D. Jakes. "Kids put athletes on pedestals a little too much," says Sanders. "We really are just human." He goes on to say, "Some of the greatest role models are found at home or in our churches."

Prime Time had his days of scoring touchdowns and dancing in the end zone. But after the stadium full of cheering fans had gone home, he was empty inside. His pursuit of power, money, and sex had not produced its perceived happiness. There was a void that no amount of adoration could fill.

His view of success changed with his commitment to follow Jesus. Deion realized that pursuing integrity and character were second only to seeking a personal relationship with God. He devoted himself to becoming a new man—a man after God's own heart and a person of great integrity.

In a similar manner the Babylonian captivity of the Jews set the stage for a truly uncommon display of integrity from Daniel and his three friends. Daniel shows us that adversity of any kind—even chastening from sin—is God's way of nourishing and strengthening the spiritual trait of integrity. Without the adversities of Babylon and his good upbringing, Daniel's integrity and that of his friends would not have shone as brightly as it did and would not have had as significant an impact on those observing their situation.

What type of adversity are you now experiencing? You may not yet understand what God is accomplishing through it, but know this: He wishes to see your character and your faith refined. Much like Deion and Daniel, we can pray for wisdom to understand God's will and the faith to trust Him through the process.

Integrity shines brightest against the backdrop of adversity.
—Anonymous

"Character is what you are in the dark."

—Dwight L. Moody

"Conscience is the inner voice which warns us that someone may be looking."

—H. L. Mencken

"Character is much easier kept than recovered."

—Thomas Paine

Chapter

Second Quarter

If you'll not settle for anything less than the best, you will be amazed at what you can do with your lives.

—Vince Lombardi

"When he goes into a restaurant, he doesn't ask for a menu, he asks for an estimate."

—Tony Kornheiser, Sportswriter, on William "The Refrigerator" Perry

26

The Big Mo: The Invisible Team Member

Avid football fans often say that one of the most exciting games ever played occurred on a cold December afternoon in 1958. The powerful New York Giants clashed with the Baltimore Colts and a young quarterback named Johnny Unitas during the first ever NFL overtime game.

In 1955 the Pittsburgh Steelers, who suggested that he was too small and too slow, cut Unitas. Finally, in the following off-season, a call came to Unitas from the Colts—they wanted to give him a tryout. They eventually signed the skinny rookie as a backup quarterback. As fate would have it, during the fourth game of the 1956 season, the starting quarterback broke his knee, opening the door for Johnny U. to do his thing. In the following years Unitas would set many records, including throwing at least one TD pass in each of forty-seven consecutive games.

On that historic day in 1958, before a roaring crowd of 64,185 in Yankee Stadium, Unitas directed the Colts to a thrilling come-from-behind 23–17 overtime victory. The ebb and flow of the game kept fans on the edge of their seats the entire time. The finicky, invisible player called "Big Mo," a.k.a. "momentum," seemed to vacillate back and forth, unable to choose a winner between the two teams.

Most coaches will tell you that embracing momentum can mean the difference between victory and defeat. There are many things that build momentum during a game. It could be as simple as the ball bouncing your way, or a spectacular achievement by a marquee player, or a previously unknown player who steps up and plays the game of his life. When these things happen, play after play, the team begins to feel confident. They tend to play with more enthusiasm and abandonment. Endorphins begin to pump into their systems, creating a natural increase in energy.

In a similar manner the Holy Spirit empowers a Christian. Through the Spirit, God gives believers all the spiritual power they need to live a victorious Christian life. When the Spirit enters the life of a new believer, new power, enduring strength, and godly wisdom are available so that he or she might serve others and grow in the knowledge of God. In Ephesians 3:20 Paul encouraged the new believers in Ephesus that God's Spirit can do far more in their lives than they could ever imagine.

Through actual experience Paul knew of the spiritual resources and power supply that only the Holy Spirit can provide. He was regularly challenged physically, emotionally, and spiritually, yet found peace and comfort in the energy of the Comforter: "We are afflicted in every way, but not crushed; perplexed, but not despairing; persecuted, but not forsaken; struck down, but not destroyed" (2 Corinthians 4:8–9 NASB). Paul's power was found in his identification with the risen Christ and the appropriation of the power of God's Spirit.

Like with the Big Mo in a game, we can win at life if we utilize the power of the Spirit. When you encounter fear, frustrations, failures, threats, or sickness, remember the Holy Spirit is your true source of strength and might. And unlike the Big Mo, which is sometimes fickle, you can count on God's Comforter to remain true to the end.

‹⬤›

[He] is able to do exceedingly abundantly beyond all that we ask or think, according to the power that works within us.
—Ephesians 3:20 NASB

"**H**urt is in the mind. You've got to make yourself tough and you've got to play when it hurts. That's when you play best, when it hurts. If you don't want to get hurt, then don't play football."

—**Harry Lombardi,** to his son Vince
when he broke his leg playing football

27

No Pain, No Gain

Much like the frustrations of a losing football season, at times life can be full of disappointments. With the advent of salary caps, free agency, and parity, teams that only a few years ago seemed unbeatable can quickly become struggling franchises.

Blame starts popping out and finger pointing begins as the press, the fans, and the management start to analyze the situation. Within days of a disappointing season, a once successful coaching staff is perhaps at risk of being terminated. Fickle fans start venting their frustrations on talk radio programs as if the host of the show had the power of the team's senior managing partner.

It's interesting to me that a corporate executive can have a bad day at work and life goes on. A stockbroker can choose the wrong investments for his clients and still remain in business. But if a starting coach, quarterback, receiver, or kicker has a bad day, millions will hear about it throughout the week.

As important as football might be to some, the fleeting grief felt from a loss or a bad season may be partially soothed with next week's win or next spring's high draft choice. Most good coaches or players who are let go because of a dismal season will usually find a team willing to give them another try.

Conversely there are individuals who feel the unrelenting pain of enduring trials: those suffering the challenges associated with fighting a terminal illness, a family abandoned by the mother of the house because she felt she needed a less stressful life, the business associate who had a major financial reversal, or the conscientious pastor who suffers endless slanderous attacks from a few disgruntled parishioners.

There are all kinds of trials and sufferings. Scripture is filled with people whose great character was molded by the amount of pain and distress they endured. From their stories we are reminded that with suffering comes the opportunity to honor, trust, obey, and know God more intimately. Peter, the longsuffering disciple, reminds us, "After you have suffered for a little while, the God of all grace . . . will Himself perfect, confirm, strengthen and establish you" (1 Peter 5:10 NASB).

While we live out our life on earth, sufferings can teach us to develop patience and perseverance. I'm thankful that in heaven we won't need to work on these traits; our primary role will be that of praising and worshiping God (Revelation 4–5). We are promised that as we learn to endure today's trials and tribulations, we can expect to receive great rewards in eternity. The greater our earthly challenges, the greater opportunity there will be to glorify God.

We read in Scripture how James and John were arguing over who would have the position of highest prestige in the kingdom of God (Matthew 20:20–23). They recognized that eternal rewards would eventually be honored. What they didn't fully grasp was the suffering they would endure to obtain such powerful positions in God's kingdom.

The Lord wants us to realize that the chief end of every trial is to provide opportunities to

- gain a greater understanding of God's mercy, kindness, goodness, love, peace, strength, comfort, and goodness;
- further develop our patience, perseverance, and compassion so that our character might be refined;
- comfort others with the love and encouragement we have received;
- obtain the satisfaction and the joy that builds our future capacity to glorify God.

Whether we experience life on a football field or at home, there will be challenges and sufferings. That's life. People who are successful in coping with suffering know that God's grace and love are sufficient to comfort and encourage them through their dilemma. God can use the familiar to teach the incredible. He can turn our nothing into something.

If we endure, we will also reign with Him.

—*2 Timothy 2:12*

> **"N**o wonder centers get confused. They're always looking at the world upside down and backwards."
>
> —**Bob Zuppke,** Former Illinois Coach

28

The Anchor at Center

Some consider offensive linemen to be big strong bodies who are not smart enough or skilled enough to play a "respectable position." In 1968, when Paul Brown took command of the expansion Cincinnati Bengals, the first player he drafted wasn't a quarterback or a running back or a defensive lineman. He selected Bob Johnson, a center from the University of Tennessee.

"With this young man," Brown said, "we have a player who will anchor our offensive line for the next decade." Johnson went on to play twelve seasons, helping the Bengals develop into a consistent contender.

I believe the inspiration for Brown's decision came from observing former University of Miami center Jim Otto. At 205 pounds, many considered Jim too small to play professional football. However, his exceptional desire, positive spirit, and keen insights into the game of football quickly propelled this unlikely player into becoming one of the NFL's greatest stars.

Upon entering the newly developed American Football Conference in 1960, Otto's dedicated work ethic inspired his fellow players. His consistency and durability is now legendary—he started every regular season game for the next fifteen years. For thirteen straight seasons, he was All-Pro, the only All-AFC center in the league's history.

As number "00" developed into a superstar, so did his team. The

Oakland Raiders' win-loss record while Jim snapped the ball was impressive: seven divisional championships in an eight-year period, plus a Super Bowl win. Jim was inducted into the Pro Football Hall of Fame on August 2, 1980. He was so well respected that he was accepted in his first year of eligibility, only the third AFC graduate to be so honored. "He loved to win. He led by example, and he set the tempo," his longtime teammate George Blanda said. "He gave the Raiders an image of hard discipline, hard work, and hard-nosed football."

To be a great center like Otto, you need to be a sure-handed ball-snapper and a superior blocker who seeks out targets far beyond the limited area immediately in front of your position. The center also has the burden of calling blocking signals for the offensive line. If he makes mental errors, the quarterback or running back has a face-to-face encounter with the defense. A first-rate center needs to have wisdom, quickness, agility, discipline, and stamina.

Because of Otto's dedication, he has been called the "Iron Man of Football." Having now endured thirty-eight repair operations, the descriptions of which could fill a medical encyclopedia, he continues to persevere. He is currently the Special Projects Coordinator and general ombudsman for the Oakland Raiders and a great spokesman for the NFL and his Lord Jesus Christ.

It's no wonder that many coaches consider the center, aside from the quarterback, as having the most important offensive position on the field. Most other linemen can concentrate solely on their assigned blocking tasks, but the center must focus on recognizing the defensive alignment, calling the appropriate blocking assignments, remembering the snap count, snapping the ball, then preparing himself both mentally and physically to take a beating from onrushing linemen and linebackers. "Knowing he's going to get blasted as soon as he snaps the ball, a center needs more mental discipline than anybody at any other position," says commentator John Madden.

Because every play except kickoffs begins with the center's snap and ends with the center determining where the next huddle will be established, there is probably not a more critical player to the functioning of the offense. Many describe the center as the anchor or foundation of the team.

So it is with a true disciple of Christ. He lines up daily to "take the shots" the world hands out, knowing that any day he may have to face hatred, bitterness, jealousy, pride, dishonesty, greed, sexual temptation, trickery, and deceit. As previously cited, Paul testified, "Our struggle is not against flesh and blood, but against the rulers, against the authorities, against the powers of this dark world and against the spiritual forces of evil in the heavenly realms" (Ephesians 6:12).

If we are to be the anchor of faithfulness and holiness at work, at home, and in our communities, we must properly prepare ourselves that we might play to win the game of life. Like the great Jim "00" Otto, we must be tough, determined, committed, and dedicated to the effort. Otto wouldn't think about going out to play a game without first studying his opponent, preparing himself mentally, putting on the proper protective gear, and spiritually committing himself to God Almighty.

While speaking to the Ephesians, Paul reminds each of us:

> [God] lavished on us ... all wisdom and understanding. And he made known to us the mystery of his will according to his good pleasure, which he purposed in Christ. (1:8–9)
> I keep asking that the God of our Lord Jesus Christ, the glorious Father, may give you the Spirit of wisdom and revelation, so that you may know him better. (1:17)
> He Himself is our peace. (2:14 NASB)
> In Him and through faith in Him we may approach God with freedom and confidence. (3:12)

Once we have studied our opponents, we must prepare ourselves through prayer, and then we must (figuratively speaking) don our protective equipment: "Put on the full armor of God so that you can take your stand against the devil's schemes" (6:11).

The protective equipment for the believer is

- the belt of truth and honesty (integrity);
- the breastplate of righteousness (good character is our defense);
- readiness to proclaim the gospel (of peace) on our feet;
- the shield of faith (being confident in our belief);
- the helmet of salvation (signifying our confidence and victory in Christ);
- the sword of the Spirit (we must fight with God's Word and strength through the presence and the power of the Holy Spirit in our lives).

Finally, we must spiritually commit ourselves to the game. Several NFL coaches I have talked with tell me they like to have committed Christians on their team because they are good role models, dependable workers, have a good work ethic, stay out of trouble, and know the meaning of sacrifice. Let's join people like Jim Otto and fight to win the victory!

Being a nose tackle [opposing the center] is like being the fire hydrant at a dog show.

—Doug Dieken, Former Brown Offensive Tackle

<blockquote>
"If Steve Young's hands are worth $40 million,
I wonder how much my rear end would go for?"

—**Trevor Matick,** Young's Center at BYU
</blockquote>

29

All Things Are Possible

Most fans have no idea of the depth of personal pain and suffering two-time NFL MVP Kurt Warner went through to become the respected and admired quarterback we see on national television.

Prior to 1995, when Warner became a Christian, he tried to fill the emptiness in his life with everything the world had to offer ... but the void remained. With regular frequency, disappointment and tragedy seemed to strike his life. The parents of his girlfriend, Brenda (now his wife), were killed when a tornado demolished their home in Mountain View, Arkansas. The couple had planned to be baptized that night but stayed home because Brenda's mother had a headache, according to *USA Today*.

Warner watched and learned of Christ's sustaining power as Brenda, a Christian, responded to the tragedy with poise and grace rather than self-pity. He also knew how she dealt with a crippling accident suffered by her son, Zachary, eight years earlier. As a lonely single parent, Brenda sat in a rocking chair next to Zachary's hospital crib for seventeen days, watching as he suffered seizures; she quoted Bible verses and asked God to perform a miracle. Although legally blind and brain-damaged, Zachary is now a fifth-grader who can read, get around fairly well, and take mainstream and special education classes.

Three months after the deaths of Brenda's parents, Kurt became a Christian. Just a few months after he proposed to Brenda, he adopted Zachary and his younger sister, Jesse. Warner continued to suffer setbacks in his career, but he faced the challenges with a new sense of peace and comfort. He knew Brenda was a special and encouraging friend and life partner that God had given him.

Warner started attending a Bible study and began to "understand what was really important in life," as he told an Internet reporter at Crosswalk.com. "I had my life and my faith, and they were two separate things. But as I began to grow in my relationship with God, I began to understand how they fit together." He now testifies that struggles were no longer a thing to dread but an opportunity for him to grow in his character while becoming more Christlike in his behavior.

In another segment I discussed the apostle Paul's teachings about *finishing strong*. I briefly mentioned the importance our attitude plays on how we view life. This is especially true when disappointment and difficulties come our way.

How many times have you been disappointed or frightened or misunderstood or personally attacked? Paul knew what it felt like to be rejected, forgotten, hated, lonely, isolated, and misconstrued. He refused to equate defeat with failure, or disappointment with lack of commitment. He finished his work, and he *finished strong*.

Paul saw his struggles not as impossibilities but as opportunities to testify to his faith in God. He regularly reminded his colleagues and persecutors, "*I can do all things through Christ who strengthens me*" (Philippians 4:13 NKJV).

A person's belief system operates much like a thermostat. How and what we believe about God, His Word, and ourselves will affect our determination to be successful and to have victory over our problems.

There are many points of focus we could consider when it comes to dealing with the challenges life brings our way. Let's look at five thoughts gleaned from Scripture on how to deal with those testing times.

First, accept God's truth concerning your life. He loves each of us and has a plan for our lives. He desires that nothing keep us from experiencing His infinite grace and affection. Our Father has equipped each one of us with a gift(s) that we are to pursue in fulfilling His plan: "He who calls you is faithful, who also will do it" (1 Thessalonians 5:24 NKJV).

Second, never give up! God will provide a way through your difficult and challenging circumstances. Keep looking for the "unlocked door" that He has provided (1 Corinthians 10:13).

Third, study God's Word, our greatest source of comfort, peace, and encouragement. As we meditate upon His truth, we will discover the tranquility and inspiration needed for effective problem solving. "How can a young man cleanse his way? By taking heed according to your word" (Psalm 119:9 NKJV).

Fourth, affirm and utilize the gifts God has given you. He wants each of us to be His representative. Whatever our talents, we are to use them to be successful in the field He has called us to serve. Paul did not shy away from his God-given abilities, and neither should we (1 Corinthians 12).

Finally, remind yourself each day and in every circumstance that we are never alone. Dear friend, God is with us through our struggles just as He was with the Warners through theirs. Our heavenly Father deeply enjoys our fellowship and desires a personal relationship with each of His children.

Whatever your tests, wherever the challenge, whoever the enemy, remember that God is the Victor! If we trust in Him who is able, we can *finish strong* in whatever tasks, circumstances, or challenges are before us.

With man this is impossible, but with God all things are possible.
—*Matthew 19:26*

30

Fumbles and Failures

On November 17, 1968, my wife and I took our humble seats in the corner of the end zone at the Oakland Coliseum to watch the celebrated New York Jets take on our hometown heroes, the Raiders. This nationally televised game became famous for its unique closing.

Perhaps one of the more famous fumbles in football history occurred with 1:05 left to play in the game with the Jets leading the Raiders by a score of 32–29. NBC, in its infinite wisdom, cut from the game to show the scheduled Sunday night movie, *Heidi*. Football didn't have the respect it now enjoys, and our culture, supposedly, was more interested in visiting Switzerland through the life of a cute little girl dressed in a frilly dress.

While some football fans around the country were making room on the couch for those in the family who enjoy less physical stuff, and others were frantically calling television stations, Raider fans at the Coliseum were being treated to one of the most exciting ninety seconds in football history.

Within the first twenty-three seconds of the preempted program, the Raiders scored a touchdown to take the lead. Then, with only forty-two seconds remaining, they recovered a fumble on the kickoff and went on to score again. Two touchdowns in less than a minute!

Needless to say, the New York coaches were visibly traumatized. As disappointed as the Jets were, NBC executives were even more disheartened to know that they'd fumbled away the opportunity to broadcast one of the most exciting comebacks ever.

Coaches work hard with players to develop in them the skills needed to protect the ball at all cost. Most NFL teams conduct a regular drill in which the runner scampers past a group of heavy-handed linemen who attempt to knock the ball away.

Fumbles, failures, goofs—whatever you call them—do strange things to a team's confidence. They can be momentum breakers and can produce lost games—both in sports and in life. On the flip side, however, when too much attention is placed upon these occasional failures, it can cost a good player his confidence and his composure.

Wendell Tyler was a gifted 49er running back obtained from the Los Angeles Rams in the early 1980s. He was extremely quick and agile, providing Joe Montana with a solid receiver option from the backfield. In 1983 and 1984 he led the team in rushing yards, and considering Roger Craig was the other running back, Tyler did very well to gain as many yards as he did.

Despite two great postseason performances—in 1983 against the Detroit Lions and in 1984 against the Miami Dolphins (which culminated in a 49er Super Bowl XIX victory)—Tyler was not invited back for a fifth season, in part because he fumbled several times.

How often have you dropped the ball? Maybe you missed a critical appointment at work. Or perhaps you forgot your child's or even your spouse's birthday. If we place too much attention on our missed opportunities, we can become ineffective and depressed.

Despite our shortcomings, God can use each of us to build His kingdom. I think too many people feel unworthy because they place too much focus upon their failures instead of on the graciousness of a loving God.

Too often we glorify Bible characters and believe that our ability to serve God is less than those "saintly" prophets and apostles of yesterday. It is encouraging to remember that our heavenly Father has equipped each one of us with special talents. He wants us to utilize these gifts rather than be overly critical of our failures. Think about how God used biblical characters despite their imperfections:

- Moses stuttered.
- David's armor didn't fit.
- John Mark was rejected by Paul.
- Hosea's wife was a prostitute.
- Amos's only training was in the school of fig-tree pruning.
- Solomon was too rich.
- Abraham was too old.
- Timothy had ulcers.
- Peter was afraid of death.
- Lazarus was dead.
- John was self-righteous.
- Naomi was a widow.
- Paul was a murderer. (So were Moses and David.)
- Jonah ran from God.
- Miriam was a gossip.
- Gideon and Thomas both doubted.
- Jeremiah was depressed and suicidal.
- Elijah was burned out.
- John the Baptist was a loudmouth.
- Martha was a worrywart.
- Samson struggled with lust.
- Did I mention that Moses had a short fuse? So did Peter, Paul—well, lots of folks did.

Aren't we glad God doesn't keep an account of our fumbles? He is quick to forgive and forget; despite a bad year He still has us in His lineup next season. He doesn't require a job interview. He doesn't hire and fire like human bosses, because He's more than our Boss. He's not prejudiced or partial, not judging, grudging, sassy or brassy, not deaf to our cry or blind to our need.

If we are totally in love with Him, if we hunger for Him more than for our next breath, He'll use us in spite of who we are, where we've been, or what we look like. Step out of your limitations into the illimitable nature of who God is.

It was He who gave some to be apostles, some to be prophets, some to be evangelists, and some to be pastors and teachers, to prepare God's people for works of service, so that the body of Christ may be built up until we all reach unity in the faith and in the knowledge of the Son of God and become mature, attaining to the whole measure of the fullness of Christ.

—Ephesians 4:11–13

31

Enduring a Loss

The January 14, 2001, AFC Playoff game between the Oakland Raiders and the Baltimore Ravens will long be remembered for the intense defensive play from both teams. The "game-stopper" came as a 300-pound Raven lineman crushed Rich Gannon to the turf in the second quarter, bringing a collective gasp to everyone watching. "The guy came out of nowhere and blindsided me," stated the All-Pro quarterback.

Another aspect of this game that will also be remembered is the courage and character Gannon demonstrated by returning to the field of play after being treated in the locker room by a team of doctors. Despite obvious pain, Rich persevered and continued to play as long as he could.

The discouragement of this day would have pressured most players into an emotional frenzy. Many in the same position would have tossed their helmets to the ground, kicked the water cooler, cussed at the coach, and made a scene. I'm sure the depth of Gannon's disappointment was great, yet he demonstrated amazing control and maturity as he left the field for the initial X-ray during a crucial series.

When I think of men who've modeled great character and endurance, the apostle Paul always comes to mind. One reason he was able to endure trials and disappointment was that he knew the physical and the emotional were far less important and less lasting than the spiritual.

Paul was able to accept physical suffering and personal disappointment because he knew his inner man (spiritual self) was being renewed daily. Paul, like Christ, was a true role model. Through the power of the Holy Spirit Paul urges all of us to "set your mind on the things above, not on the things that are on earth" (Colossians 3:2 NASB).

God's Word assures us that He will provide all the strength we need to endure, even if it is the tough loss of a championship game. Gannon, his teammates, fans, and all of us can draw comfort from the words of a wise prophet:

"Don't you yet understand? Don't you know by now that the everlasting God, the Creator of the farthest parts of the earth, never grows faint or weary? No one can fathom the depths of his understanding. He gives power to the tired and worn out, and strength to the weak. Even the youths shall be exhausted, and the young men will all give up. But they that wait upon the Lord shall renew their strength. They shall mount up with wings like eagles; they shall run and not be weary; they shall walk and not faint" (Isaiah 40:28–31 TLB).

Momentary, light affliction is producing for us an eternal weight of glory far beyond all comparison.

—*2 Corinthians 4:17* NASB

> "**E**very year we keep going to a minor bowl. If they have a Soybean Bowl next year, we'll probably be at that."

> —**Tony Mason,** Former University of Cincinnati Coach

32

Number One Ranking

For decades folks have pondered how to properly rank college football teams. With the growing media dollars available to the colleges making Bowl Championship Series (BCS) games, the evaluation and selection process has fallen under much scrutiny. Big bucks are at stake for the colleges that obtain boasting rights by being considered for prestigious bowl games.

The most critical decisions on ranking often come around mid-November when bowl invitations are being sent to worthy teams. In the past organizing committees have sometimes given in to social pressure or media hype, causing them to make poor selections. At the end of the 2000 bowl season the Bowl Championship Series Committee was pelted with criticism and all but tarred, feathered, and run out of town over the fact that with all the computer capacity known to humankind they somehow could not manage to get the two correct teams into the 2000 mythical national championship game.

According to the Sports section in *USA Today* on October 19, 2001, "After being appropriately chastened, the BCS boys went back to the drawing board and tinkered and tweaked and replaced one computer geek with another and now, finally, are ready to unveil their new and improved BCS system."

The only problem with the new system is you have to have a Ph.D. from

MIT to make sense of it. The new (2001) BCS formula goes something like this: The Poll Rankings from AP, *USA Today*, and ESPN + Myriad Computer Rankings + Schedule Strength From Win-Loss Record of Opponents + Record, Including Number of Losses—Quality Wins Against Teams Ranked Among the Top 15 Your BCS Ranking.

I'm sure there are many statisticians who relish the opportunity to play with their computers and calculators if only to argue about who is number one. However, when it comes to the bottom line, it doesn't matter what others think of a team's play but rather how each member of a team performs to the best of his ability.

I'm very content to take wise counsel from one of the best coaches ever to be connected with the game. While his remarks were given to a professional team, I think most college coaches and the BCS committee could agree with his philosophy.

Vince Lombardi passed along these words to the Green Bay Packers about how to judge who is really *number one*:

> Winning is not a sometime thing; it's an all-the-time thing. You don't win once in a while, you don't do things right once in a while, you do them right all the time. Winning is a habit. Unfortunately, so is losing. . . .
>
> It's a reality of life that men are competitive, and the most competitive games draw the most competitive men. That's why they're there—to compete. They know the rules and the objectives when they get in the game. The objective is to win—fairly, squarely, decently, by the rules—but to win.
>
> And in truth, I've never known a man worth his salt who in the long run, deep down in his heart, didn't appreciate the grind, the discipline. There is something in good men that really yearns for, needs, discipline and the harsh reality of head-to-head combat.
>
> I don't say these things because I believe in the 'brute' nature of man or that men must be brutalized to be combative. I believe in God, and I believe in human decency. But I firmly believe that any man's finest hour—his greatest fulfillment to all he holds dear—is that moment when he has worked his heart out in a good cause and lies exhausted on the field of battle—victorious.

In much the same way a good coach inspires his team, the apostle Paul gave confidence to his band of followers. His task was to uplift and encourage thousands of new converts with a message of hope and eternal life through belief in our resurrected Savior, the Lord Jesus Christ.

Of special concern to Paul was his small team of disciples who looked to him for guidance. During his fourth missionary journey, Paul instructed Timothy to care for the church at Ephesus. He wanted Timothy to be his representative and to carry out the special work Paul left to his keeping. With his life constantly threatened, Paul knew his time with his disciples might be cut short.

Like Coach Lombardi, Paul was inspired to give his team a parting speech that still rings true for today's disciples:

> O Timothy, you are God's man. Run from all these evil things, and work instead at what is right and good, learning to trust him and love others and to be patient and gentle. *Fight* on for God. Hold tightly to the eternal life that God has given you and that you have confessed with such a ringing confession before many witnesses. I command you before God, who gives life to all, and before Christ Jesus, who gave a fearless testimony before Pontius Pilate, that you fulfill all he has told you to do so that no one can find fault with you from now until our Lord Jesus Christ returns.
>
> For in due season Christ will be revealed from heaven by the blessed and only Almighty God, the King of kings and Lord of lords, who alone can never die, who lives in light so terrible that no human being can approach him. No mere man has ever seen him nor ever will. Unto him be honor and everlasting power and dominion forever and ever. Amen. (1 Timothy 6:11–16, TLB, emphasis added)

Let's fight on and become victorious!

To win the contest you must deny yourselves many things that would keep you from doing your best. An athlete goes to all this trouble just to win a blue ribbon or a silver cup, but we do it for a heavenly reward that never disappears.

—1 Corinthians 9:25 TLB

> **"I** give the same half-time speech over and over. It works best when my players are better than the other coach's players."

> —**Chuck Mills,** Former Wake Forest Coach

33

Don't Miss Half Time

Half time is to a football game what intermission is to fine opera. It's a chance for the participants to catch their breath and reevaluate personal goals. In a football situation, coaches make timely adjustments in the game plan and modify their offensive and defensive alignments to take better advantage of their opponent's weaknesses.

Unlike what we occasionally see on video clips, there usually isn't much in the way of a "Knute Rockne" speech by most head coaches. Once they exit the field, players grab a sports beverage and some energy bars as a quick snack while they sit down and listen to their position coaches. The half-time locker room is broken down into a number of small groups having intense discussions about diagrams and computer pictures that illustrate the opponent's alignments. Players talk about any problems they have with specific assignments and how they can take advantage of their opponent's limitations.

While the marching bands and baton twirlers take their final bow, the head coach usually reminds the players about the importance of the game and encourages everyone to play to his potential. This professional approach should not minimize the importance emotion plays in the game of football. Even so, at a professional level most players are pretty well energized with pride (and also incentive clauses in their contracts for specific individual accomplishments).

In 1928 Notre Dame's head coach, Knute Rockne, gave his famous challenge "Win one for the Gipper" to motivate his players to leave it all on the field. It had its effect: Notre Dame won over a very tough Army team 12–6 on a touchdown pass from Butch Niemiec to Johnny O'Brien in the closing minutes of the game.

A few years before, George Gipp was a quiet and unassuming triple threat (runner, passer, and kicker) for Notre Dame. He had great confidence and inspired others with his dedicated efforts. Rockne later recalled, "I learned very early to place full confidence in his self-confidence." Had there been a Heisman Trophy that year, most coaches felt George Gipp would have received it.

In 1920 Notre Dame finished its season with a 25–0 victory over Michigan State, but their dedicated Gipp was in the college infirmary at South Bend with a life-threatening infection. Antibiotic drugs had not yet been developed, and Gipp's condition was worsening by the day. In the last few hours before his passing, Coach Rockne made one of his daily visits to see Gipp. The lanky collegian All-Star looked into his coach's eyes and said, "Someday in a tough game, ask the players to win one for the Gipper."

For eight years Rockne thought about the proper time to encourage his players with the deathbed words of this dedicated athlete. Many on the 1928 Notre Dame team knew of George Gipp and had actually been in grammar school with the legendary running back. The motivation and inspiration of Rockne's famous locker room words helped guide Notre Dame to a victory and won the hearts of millions of future fans.

We all need to take time to be inspired and to restore our spiritual passion. All of us need opportunity to reassess our lives and to refocus priorities. We live in a hurried culture with instant everything. Stress abounds in the workplace as well as in many homes. Enough never seems to be enough in a culture that has grown weary in its demands and expectations. Our attention can easily become riveted on the temporal and the material as we desperately seek to provide a "better way of life" for our families. We have now learned that this hurried burnout is the common cause of many diseases plaguing our nation.

As for all our concerns, the Bible provides great inspiration and counsel on how to deal with our busy pace. Even when our work has eternal value, we can overtax ourselves by developing a "Messiah complex."

Such was the case in the first few months of the disciples' ministry experience. Christ trained them over a three-year period and provided spiritual truth to guide them on their missionary journeys. They saw many of Christ's miracles and became ready to accept the challenges that ministry brings. Jesus sent them out in pairs so that they could encourage one another while they reached people with the Good News.

According to the gospel of Mark, the disciples had been teaching, preaching, and healing throughout the countryside. After laboring day and night, they received some devastating information. Their friend John the Baptist had been beheaded. The exhausted and emotionally troubled group now needed the comfort and companionship of their Lord.

They returned to the Galilee area and found Jesus. My Bible is open to Mark 6:31–32, where we pick up the story: "Then, because so many people were coming and going that they did not even have a chance to eat, he (Jesus) said to them, 'Come with me by yourselves to a quiet place and get some rest.' So they went away by themselves in a boat to a solitary place."

Knowing that at least eight of the twelve disciples loved to fish, I think climbing into their boats to enjoy some quiet time relaxing, fishing, resting, and restoring their spiritual passion with their Savior was a natural for them.

Scripture encourages us to take regular "half-time breaks" to be alone with God. We are to catch our spiritual breath by focusing upon His goodness, mercy, love, power, encouragement, grace, and kindness. God's Word commands us to periodically surrender the hectic pace of everyday life and find that quiet spot where the distractions and tensions of our environment can be screened out.

The first three verses of Psalm 23 give us a good progression to follow.

- *"The Lord is my shepherd, I shall not be in want"* (v. 1). Recognize that without Jesus as Lord of your life you cannot receive His strength and comfort.
- *"He makes me lie down in green pastures"* (v. 2a). There are times when we need to physically rest. We need to lie down and recharge our chemical, emotional, and spiritual batteries.
- *"He leads me beside quiet waters"* (v. 2b). Sheep can't rest or be renewed by trying to drink from the turbulent part of the stream. They get nervous, edgy, and frightened around the noise and confusion of raging waters. In a similar manner, we cannot always revive our spirit

by seeking to fellowship with God Almighty in the hectic environment of a congested office or busy airport. Seek out those quiet places to fellowship with God. If you can't find a relaxing open space, then seek a small place of solitude.

- *"He restores my soul"* (v. 3a). Note the progression. After we identify and accept the lordship of Christ in our lives, after we lie down and physically rest, and after we find a quiet place to meditate and pray—then we can be restored.
- *"He guides me in paths of righteousness"* (v. 3b). After we are restored, then God can guide and direct our paths. We can more clearly hear His whispers and focus upon His will for our lives.

I think I just heard the half-time whistle blow. How about you? The "half-time experience" rejuvenated the disciples' lives in order that they could be more effective in their work and relationships. When is your next half time?

◀🏈▶

 Be still, and know that I am God.

—Psalm 46:10

"A little integrity is better than any career."

—Ralph Waldo Emerson

"Society does nominally estimate men by their talents—but really feels and knows them by their characters."

—Henry David Thoreau

Chapter

Half-Time Report

I'm just a plowhand from Arkansas, but I
have learned how to hold a team
together. How to lift some men up, how
to calm down others, until finally they've
got one heartbeat together: a team.
There are just three things I'd ever say:
"If anything goes bad, I did it. If anything
goes semi-good, then we did it. If
anything goes real good, then you did it."

—Bear Bryant

> "John [Madden] is the one man who doesn't let
> success go to his clothes."
>
> —Mike Ditka

34

The Strongest Muscle

One of my favorite football stories underscores the importance of encouragement. Motivation often occurs out of the huddle of inspiration. In football, there was probably no greater leader and encourager than Green Bay Hall-of-Fame quarterback Bart Starr. When he was in his prime there was none better. He utilized his mind and voice to prompt and inspire his team.

While football was a very important part of Starr's life, his family was his central focus. It's interesting to note that many successful football players also have a loving and supportive family that encourages and inspires *them* during the tough times.

During the season Starr would try to stay updated with his kids' activities by weekly reviewing their homework and tests. If a paper was particularly good he would tape a dime to the work and write a note saying, "I love you and I'm proud of you!"

In 1965 Starr had a bad outing against the St. Louis Cardinals. It was a nationally televised game, and much of America's football audience was watching. The Green Bay QB fumbled a few times, and in the final minutes he threw an interception that cost his team the victory. That night the team flew back to Green Bay. Late in the evening he got home only to find a note placed on the refrigerator door. It read, "Dad, I saw your game today. I want you to know I love you and I'm still proud of you." Signed, Bart Jr.

The words of encouragement from his young son had their influence on Bart, his family, and the Green Bay Packers. He realized the impact that timely comforting remarks could have on a person's perspective. Unfortunately, as Bart Jr. matured he allowed peer pressure to change his positive outlook on life. He did not stay with the uplifting concepts his dad taught.

Articulating an encouraging attitude can motivate people in a special way. Our tongues are but a little muscle, yet they have enormous power for both good and evil. In the book of Proverbs we find many references dealing with the positive use of our tongue; for instance, "Reckless words pierce like a sword, but the tongue of the wise brings healing" (12:18); "He who guards his mouth and his tongue keeps himself from calamity" (21:23).

Webster's gives this definition of encouragement: "To inspire with courage ... to help or foster." However, encouraging others is counter to what our society projects. Critics and scoffers abound. When we aren't at the top of our game or our business, there are many who will doubt and be cynical. We must remember that Jesus came to encourage us—the Lord came to "set free those who are downtrodden" (Luke 4:18 NASB).

The following is adapted from the writings of Oz Hillman. Let's think about how our tongues can be used for encouragement and motivation.

> *The tongue has the power of life and death, and those who love it will eat its fruit.* (Proverbs 18:21)

Words have the power to motivate or destroy. Energize or deflate. Inspire or create despair. Many a successful executive can remember the time his father failed to give affirmation to him as a child. The result was either overachievement to prove his worth or underachievement to prove he was right.

Many a wife has lost her ability to love because of a critical husband. Many a husband has left a marriage because of words of disrespect and ungratefulness. Many an athlete has not performed to his/her ultimate capacity because a coach could not evaluate without attacking the person's character or self-image. Stories abound to the power of words. There are just as many stories of those that have been encouraged, challenged, and comforted with words that made a difference in their life.

Jesus knew the power of words. He used parables to convey the principles of God's kingdom. He used words of forgiveness and mercy. He used words to challenge. He used words to inspire His disciples to miraculous faith.

I believe it is especially significant that during Christ's ministry, God chose two critical times to express His encouragement and love for His Son: Matthew 3:16–17 (John baptizing Jesus), and Matthew 17:3–5 (Christ's transfiguration). Both times God said to His only begotten Son, "I LOVE YOU; I'M PROUD OF YOU!" (author's paraphrase of "This is my Son, whom I love; with him I am well pleased").

Do your words give life? Do they inspire and challenge others to greatness? Who does God want you to encourage through your words today? Choose to affirm someone close to you.

◀▥▶

The tongue is a small part of the body, but it makes great boasts. Consider what a great forest is set on fire by a small spark. The tongue also is a fire, a world of evil among the parts of the body. It corrupts the whole person, sets the whole course of his life on fire, and is itself set on fire by hell. All kinds of animals, birds, reptiles and creatures of the sea are being tamed and have been tamed by man, but no man can tame the tongue. It is a restless evil, full of deadly poison. With the tongue we praise our Lord and Father, and with it we curse men, who have been made in God's likeness. Out of the same mouth come praise and cursing.

—James 3:5–10

"**E**very time I tackle Jim Brown I hear a dice game going on in my mouth."

—Don Burroughs

35

Everyone Has a Role

I've asked this question already: Are you a spectator or a participant? Football stadiums are filled with millions of folks who sit comfortably munching favorite snacks while watching others use their gifts and talents in pursuit of a goal. It's amazing to watch players work so hard through the challenges.

Each player toils at his job, hoping to win his individual battles. There are times when it seems the energy and tension on the field is almost palpable. Each player brings a dynamic to the game: for some it's about intimidation; for others it's a quiet but powerful exercise of God-given abilities; with a few players the battle is won through analysis and applied wisdom.

The spectators also provide entertainment. Some filled with exuberance, and maybe a few too many beers, voice their approval or disapproval with deafening yells or shouts of joy. Others sit calmly waving their team's banner. And we can't overlook those spectators that get so involved in the game they actually dress up in costume, making sure to spread an ample supply of war paint on any exposed flesh. This prepares them for their role in winning the game.

The totals on the scoreboard can at times be overshadowed by the personal battles on the field. Along the sidelines, you are up close and personal, while feeling the intensity and understanding the personal suffering players experience.

The Christian experience is a great deal like the game of football. While the battle between good and evil is waging within families, in the workplace, and in the hearts of those who don't yet know the love, peace, and comfort God can provide, many Christians sit by calmly, watching events unfold. Until you become personally engaged in the struggles life brings, or make yourself available to help others who are hurting, you can't really appreciate pain.

Unfortunately, too many Christians find themselves merely spectators of life. They assume that full-time pastors and missionaries are the only ones charged with the responsibilities of ministering to others. The tragedy of September 11, 2001, in New York, Washington, D.C., and Pennsylvania, woke people up to the fact that as a nation, or as a community, or as a family, we need to get involved in helping others.

Throughout the New Testament we read of God's desire that each person fully utilize his gifts and talents to serve others. When we bury our treasured abilities, we make a grave mistake. Such was the case with an old violin collector named Luigi Tarisio, who took great pride in searching out and purchasing rare and unusual instruments. No one really knew about his obsession until he passed away. When his home was inspected and the attic opened to appraise his estate, 246 valuable violins were found.

One of the most expensive violins was hidden in an old dresser drawer. It was a rare Stradivarius that probably had not been played in 147 years. The grand instrument was literally rotting away. Tarisio had selfishly robbed the world of beautiful music and wonderful treasures.

God has given each of us unique spiritual gifts, aptitudes, abilities, and talents (read 1 Corinthians 12 and Romans 12). No two people are the same. What you might think is a common talent may in fact be a uniquely shaped personal trait that can be of real encouragement to others. We can rob ourselves as well as others of a wonder-filled life by hiding our gifts in a "humble" personality. God expects us to refine and perfect our gifts through practice and participation rather than simply being a spectator. He wants us to share our talents.

Just as a football game can stimulate a crowd of fans to a happy experience, so can you bring joy and encouragement to others as you use your God-given treasures. What is your spiritual gift (e.g., hospitality, giving, teaching, mercy, exhortation, discernment, wisdom)? In 2 Timothy 1:6, we are encouraged to fan the flame of passion as we develop our abilities. Let's not become so earthly minded that we fail to use the gifts designed with eternal value. Become a participant!

Neglect not the gift that is in thee.

—*1 Timothy 4:14* KJV

"Joe Montana is as cool as the other side of the pillow."

—Wayne Walker, 49er Broadcaster

36
Hey Coach!!!

Searching through football annals, you will come across names of the great coaches: Amos Alonzo Stagg, Knute Rockne, John Heisman, Paul Brown, Vince Lombardi, George Allen, Weeb Ewbank, Sid Gilman, Bill Walsh, Tom Landry. These coaches inspired and directed many players to develop fully and utilize their God-given talents to help lead their teams to victory.

Webster's New World Dictionary describes a coach as "the person who is in overall charge of a team and the strategy in games, the person who instructs and trains others." Today's head coach is more than a good football strategist or educator. He must be a multitalented individual with nerves of steel, the passion of an evangelist, the drive of the apostle Paul, the wisdom of Solomon, the patience of Job, the leadership abilities of a five-star general, the communication skills of a politician, the compassion of a pastor, the applied psychology of a therapist, the persuasion skills of a salesman, and the willingness to work long hours. Most important, he must have a loving, patient family who will support and encourage him through his darkest hours.

What possesses a man to become a head coach? Some evolve into the position because they enjoyed the game as a player and want to continue in the sport. Many coaches started off in high school or college as an assistant. A few came from the ranks of business.

Today the best coaches seem to be guys who played a limited amount of college or pro ball but have always desired to lead and direct others to success. They are men who love the game and are full of passion.

A successful coach will surround himself with successful people who share his work ethic, values, philosophy, and fervor for the game. A great coach is an innovator and visionary seeking to add new wrinkles to the game in order to test his opponents' playmaking abilities.

Notre Dame's legendary Knute Rockne was such a man. He was not only known for his ability to add excitement to the game but also for his strength as a communicator. He explained new concepts to his players in an understandable way. When illustrations were needed, you would find him on the field demonstrating the techniques. He knew when to speak and when to wait. He was a motivator and encourager of men.

Some would say great coaches are born into the position. Such was the case of a young Jon Gruden. His dad, Jim, now a consultant to the San Francisco 49ers, was the running backs' coach at Notre Dame during the glory years of Joe Montana. He would regularly take his son to the games.

As a quarterback for his freshman high school team, Jon would study how the coaches worked with Montana. Even at an early age, Jon learned the sport from the inside out. His dad would give him pointers from the coach's perspective and teach him about the game as a coach would understand it. The sponge-like mind of the bright lad soaked up the various playmaking strategies of many great coaches of that day.

While Jon enjoyed football, he hadn't yet developed that unique drive that would later shape his intense coaching style. His dad could coach him on the fundamentals, but it would be up to Jon to cultivate his passion for the game.

In January 1978 the Fighting Irish took the field at the Cotton Bowl against a powerful University of Houston team. An unseasonable cold front had hit Texas, creating a major ice storm. The temperature at game time was below freezing with a serious wind-chill factor.

Houston got off to a big lead and seemed to stifle the talented Notre Dame quarterback. Montana became so cold that his body started to go into hypothermia, and he had to leave the game. "Joe was so weak he couldn't even stand up," recalls Gruden. "As a spectator, I was cold, hungry, disgusted, and felt let down that my favorite team and quarterback were not doing well." Jon remembers looking at the scoreboard in the latter part of the third quarter to see his dad's Fighting Irish on the losing end of a 34–12 score.

Jon decided he'd had enough, and he left to go sit in the warm bus until the game ended.

Just about the time his frostbitten nose began to thaw out, a little old lady boarded the bus. She was an avid fan and had ridden the bus to the game with the team and other rooters. She leaned over to Gruden and said, "I think that was the most exciting game I've ever witnessed!" Jon awoke from his daze and said, "What do you mean, exciting? Notre Dame was losing!" The elderly lady politely said, "Oh, my dear young man, I think you may have left a little early. Notre Dame scored three times in the last quarter, winning the game by one point."

After Jon picked himself up off the bus floor, he learned that after taking in some hot chicken soup and reviving his body, Joe Montana went back into the game and threw three touchdown passes as well as engineering two successful two-point conversions.

From that day onward Jon adopted a never-say-quit attitude about the game of football and the game of life. He realized the truth of the old adage "The game isn't over until it's over." This experience taught him many lessons about perseverance and patience.

Even though he was an undersized college player, quarterback Jon Gruden helped lead his University of Dayton, Ohio, team to a 24–7 record in his three varsity years. Upon graduating with a communications major, he began coaching under such dynamic head coaches as Paul Hackett, Ray Rhodes, Mike Holmgren, and George Seifert. His development as a head coach under the guidance of a creative and talented owner, Al Davis, has also impacted his coaching style and passion for the game. Coach Holmgren says this about the talented young Gruden: "Jon is a very gifted coach. When you combine his passion with a very, very bright mind—you have a coach that is very tough to beat."

Jon is currently the youngest head coach in the NFL but has the knowledge, desire, and passion that put him at the head of his class. Many believe that guys like Gruden, Steve Mariucci of the 49ers, and Herman Edwards of the Jets are the prototype head coaches that we will see more of in this new millennium.

The primary quality that drives perseverance is passion. When Jon Gruden discovered the perseverance and the passion for competing, he became a different player and ultimately a great coach. In a similar manner a disciple must have passion for his work.

Nothing challenges a person more than seeing a believer truly excited and committed about his faith. Gordon MacDonald, in his encouraging book *Restoring Your Spiritual Passion*, observes:

> Passion—the kind that causes some to excel beyond anyone else—dulls one's sense of fatigue, pain, and the need for pleasure or even well-being. Passion leads some to pay incredible prices to reach a goal of some sort. . . . A passion is necessary in the performance of Christian faith.

From the teachings of the apostle Paul we can assume that he would have made a great football coach. He was fiery and full of passion. Read his words again and see if you agree: "But one thing I do: Forgetting what is behind and straining toward what is ahead, I press on toward the goal to win the prize for which God has called me heavenward in Christ Jesus" (Philippians 3:13–14).

While football has its highs, nothing compares to the passion one experiences when he receives Christ into his heart. Like the healed man on the steps of the temple in Jerusalem (Acts 3:8), a new believer becomes focused and full of joy.

Motivation is not contingent upon winning or losing. Most committed Christian athletes come to every game prepared and dedicated to utilize their abilities to the fullest because they are no longer just playing for the coach, or the owner, or a paycheck, but for the glory of the Lord Jesus Christ. They want to persevere and to succeed.

Most coaches I know tell me that Christian athletes out-perform and last longer in the NFL than those who don't know Christ as their Savior. A committed Christian is someone who is so filled with the joy of living a dedicated life that he no longer has time to be derailed with the temptations and distractions that plague most athletes.

Just knowing about the need for passion and perseverance is not enough. One must be willing to apply the lessons learned and actively participate in the discipling process. A good coach must not only know the game of football but also be willing to demonstrate it to his athletes. He must be willing to fully commit himself to the challenge of the game and the mentoring of his players.

And so it is with the disciple of Christ. We must be properly prepared with a positive strategy and competitive desire to encourage others to live a victorious life. We will be excited and have a real passion for the truth that is within us. As Paul said, "Be made new in the attitude of your minds" (Ephesians 4:23) so that we can model a Christlike character.

A mature Christian does not preclude passion but learns to control or channel his emotions in a rational manner. He uses his passion as an engine to propel his spiritual boat and to encourage others in their faith. Even the greatest coach or disciple must have a balanced life. If we are to effectively motivate and inspire others, we must be continually filled with the power of the Holy Spirit. This can only happen through rest, prayer, meditation, fellowship, the study of God's Word, and the encouragement of a loving family. To receive this we must make time to seek God. According to God's Word, our number one goal should be *to know Him and to make Him known.* All else, including a Super Bowl win, is secondary.

Throughout the Gospels, we witness Christ withdrawing from the multitudes to be alone with the Father. He regularly recharged His spiritual batteries through prayer and mediation. While being driven by His passion and mission "to seek and to save what was lost" (Luke 19:10), He was guided by a prudent spirit of control and an internal balance. This is a model for which all of us should strive.

A passion is necessary in the performance of Christian faith.
—Gordon MacDonald

> **"I** would rather sandpaper a bobcat's butt in a phone booth than be tackled by Fredd."
>
> —**Bryan Millard,** Former Seahawk Guard,
> on Fredd Young

37

The QB of the Defense

Few words can intimidate an NFL quarterback, but one such word is *blitz*. Combine that word with names like Lawrence Taylor, Dick Butkus, Jack Lambert, Sam Huff, Ray Nitschke, Joe Schmidt, Bill George, Ray Lewis, and Junior Seau, and you have the heartbeat of a defense.

The middle linebacker is to a defense what the quarterback is to an offense. He is the playmaker, the one everyone looks to for guidance, inspiration, and advice. He is the coach's eyes and ears on defense.

The linebacker must be one of the most gifted athletes on the field. Whatever the offensive or defensive scheme, he must provide a triple threat: He must be quick enough to cover a running back on a short pass route, he must rush the passer while fending off the blocks of the big offensive linemen, and he must be able to stack up a running play that may take him from sideline to sideline.

To do this well, a linebacker must have great vision (be able to see the entire field of action), be tough and strong, be durable, and have great intuition. The enduring middle linebacker for the Oakland Raiders is one such player: Greg "Beek" Biekert. The media guide says this about him: "Intense, physical, and experienced performer with exceptional knowledge of the game." In 2000 he led his team in tackles for the third straight season with 126. After playing four years at Colorado State, Biekert was voted MVP as a senior and received All-American Honorable Mention for his inspiring play.

As I have interviewed running backs that have lined up against "Beek," they testify to his toughness by stating, "Hitting Greg is like running up against a rock wall—his feet don't move—he's planted."

In the 2000 season, Biekert's ability to know what is going to happen before it does saved the game for the Raiders against a very tough and offense-minded Colts team. Indianapolis jumped off to a 21–0 lead and seemed to have the Oakland defense thoroughly confused. However, during the second quarter Biekert identified some small but important clues to QB Peyton Manning's play-calling, and at half time he told his defensive coordinator of his discovery. The coordinator told Biekert he had the green light to do some free-lancing on any plays for which he could predict results. Biekert's intuition took over as he and his teammates shut down the powerful Colt offense and eventually won the critical game in the final minutes, 38–31.

Biekert would be the first to admit that his instincts played a prominent role. A great linebacker *must* have great instincts. While offensive players key off of voice commands, defensive players take their cues from what they see (ball movement, shifts, etc.), what they feel (body reaction of an opponent), and what they think might happen (instinct). It's pure intuition that tells a linebacker when to go and where to go.

According to defensive line coach Mike Waufle and fullback John Ritchie, "Beek can cause you more problems in the preparation of an offensive game plan than almost any other player. A tough, mobile middle linebacker like Beek can produce a lot of sleepless nights for offensive coordinators."

A good linebacker knows that every offensive alignment brings a certain strength and weakness. Depending on the defensive formation, they can either overplay the opponent's strength or prey upon their weakness.

When talking about linebackers, *Sports Illustrated* writer Rick Telander says, "Pain is something that separates linebackers from everyone else on the field—both dishing it out and receiving it." One of Biekert's role models on and off the field was the legendary Mike Singletary: "He was tough as nails and really knew how to intimidate people."

Former Bears coach Mike Ditka was a real believer in tough linebackers. He once asked Mike Singletary, "When's the last time you broke a helmet?" When Singletary replied that it had been a while, Ditka challenged him, "I want to hear one break." While playing at Baylor University, Singletary broke sixteen helmets, all of them his own.

At times Christians are called upon to play tough. When it comes to dealing with sin that could impact our loved ones or ourselves, God wants us to knock it down before it gets started. A linebacker's training and discipline is such that the battle on the field becomes natural—he tries to anticipate and prepares himself for the hit. So it is with a Christian. We must immerse ourselves in God's Word and train ourselves in His ways so that our reaction to sin becomes intuitive. Preparation is the key.

If anybody does sin, we have one who speaks to the Father in our defense—Jesus Christ, the Righteous One.

—1 John 2:1

> "My players can wear their hair as long as they want and dress any way they want. That is, if they can pay their own tuition."
>
> —**Eddie Robinson,** Former Grambling State Coach

38

Behind the Coach's Door

Bobby Bowden started off his coaching career by taking a great deal of criticism from his players, college alumni, sports fans, and the ever-judgmental media. Some passionate fans even demonstrated their frustration with the new coach by burning him in effigy. Coach Bowden struggled through those first few years and learned the importance of character-building seasons.

Today Bobby Bowden is one of the most successful coaches in college football. His 1999 Florida State Seminoles became the first college team to begin the year ranked No. 1 in the AP poll and maintain that ranking throughout the entire season.

Bowden's Christian faith plays a big part in his coaching philosophy and is always being tested. Such was the case when Heisman Trophy candidate Peter Warrick was arrested with another teammate for theft from a Tallahassee department store.

Many folks wondered how the great Bowden would handle this difficult situation and if he would dismiss his star player from the team. He struggled with the decision as to the appropriate reaction and prayed for guidance.

Bowden did what he does best: He modeled to his wayward athlete a spirit of grace mixed with some fatherly advice and discipline. Warrick was suspended for a few games and given time to think about his behavior. While many encouraged the coach to be more severe, he decided to show the young man what grace was all about.

"I feel like I have a responsibility to these kids, not just academically and athletically, but also spiritually," Bowden says. "I want them to leave here knowing about the Lord." Bowden knows that temptations can and often will get in the way of a person's career. Our moral values, cultural experience, and parenting have much to do with how we respond to a specific trial. He also hopes that each young person in his program will walk away with a greater understanding and appreciation of Jesus if they experience His love and grace from a Christian coach.

"I'm just trying to learn from my mistakes and move on," said the grateful Warrick, now with the Cincinnati Bengals. Undoubtedly Bowden's willingness to give him another chance resulted in a more mature athlete who ultimately led his team to the national championship title, winning the MVP trophy.

Coach Bowden is also aware that each person has the choice of whether he will accept or reject the modeling and mentoring he receives. Despite his best efforts and the encouragement players can receive from Bible study, there are some that just have to learn life the hard way.

An old Puritan pastor once said, "Troubles are often the tools by which God fashions us for better things." God's Word helps us understand that dealing with life's challenges is what helps produce great character.

> Not only so, but we also rejoice in our sufferings, because we know that suffering produces perseverance; perseverance, character; and character, hope. And hope does not disappoint us, because God has poured out his love into our hearts by the Holy Spirit, whom he has given us. (Romans 5:3–5)

The disciple who probably knew Christ best and undoubtedly had good insight on how to deal with challenges was his half brother James, who tells us that trials are a part of life and that it is a testing of our faith. We need to persevere, because when we stand the test we will receive the crown of life (eternal peace and great character) that God has promised (James 1:2–12).

When I think about how we should persevere, I'm reminded of the persistence of a dandelion. I have seen construction workers build a driveway that includes two inches of asphalt placed on top of four inches of crushed rock only to have a dandelion seed germinate and push through the entire mass. The wildflower struggles through each layer, pushing its roots deeper and deeper to gain strength from the nutrients of the soil so that it can ultimately break through to the life-giving sunlight.

For Christians, our struggles and failures can at times be consuming. But like the dandelion, we are called to root our spirits in God's Word so that we can ultimately push toward the Sonlight (Christ), who will fill us with the strength to press on in our work.

Hopefully this is a lesson Peter Warrick has learned and will carry with him the rest of his life. One thing we can take from this story is to know that there are people, like Coach Bowden, who will offer grace if we ask for forgiveness and help.

To extend grace (undeserved favor) to someone is to give one of the most precious gifts you can offer. Don't be afraid to forgive—it might even produce an MVP.

I have told you these things, so that in me you may have peace. In this world you will have trouble. But take heart! I have overcome the world.

—*John 16:33*

"The silver and black [Raiders] used to leave opponents black and blue. Their positions on defense were tackle, linebacker, cornerback, and armed robber. Not only were their bites worse than their barks, they could kill with their breath."

—**Mike Downey**, Sports Columnist

39

Getting After It

Every quarterback has his own way of motivating a team. Some guys, like Kenny Stabler, felt the way to a man's heart was to take him out for a cold one. Quarterbacks like Y. A. Tittle, Johnny Unitas, Roger Staubach, and Joe Montana used their maturity and their leadership skills to guide and direct their players. Some, like Oakland Raider Rich Gannon, use a more direct approach by occasionally getting in the face of their teammates.

In the October 15, 2001 issue, *Sports Illustrated*'s Michael Silver did a great job discussing the work ethic that makes Gannon one of the league's top quarterbacks. With fourteen years' experience in the NFL, Rich has been with four different teams. During this time he has become wise in perceiving what it takes to motivate others.

Only two years younger than his former head coach, Jon Gruden, Rich serves as a de facto den mother to some of the less focused and immature guys on the team. Gannon says in his interview with *Sports Illustrated*, "When I got to the Raiders, guys were showing up late to practice and meetings, and missing curfew, among other problems. I was used to an organized, disciplined system."

The area next to the quarterback's office had several pool tables and a pop-a-shot basketball hoop, plus a host of video games to keep the athletes entertained between meetings. Late in the 1999 season, just before a critical game, Rich had had enough with the partying: "It sounded like recess at an elementary school." He moved into the lounge and confiscated all the pool balls, unplugging the pop-a-shot basketball hoop and video machines and exiting the room with a frown.

That following Monday he stood before the team and gave a memorable talk about the importance of being focused and professional in their jobs. He discussed the significance of teamwork and how each man must be properly prepared for the battle. This speech was later commemorated on a specially designed T-shirt with a new Raider logo featuring Rich's face in the center of the shield.

Gannon's intensity has caught on. He points to players like Steve Wisniewski, Tim Brown, Greg Biekert, and Russell Maryland, who shared his desire to model the team's motto of "Pride and Poise." With the addition of players like Jerry Rice and Trace Armstrong, Rich now has others who share his enthusiasm for getting the job done right.

Gannon's work ethic started early. He recalls his parents saying, "Rich, don't sit in the back row where all the dummies sit. You sit in the front row, where you can learn." Throughout his football career he has endeavored to sit in the front row. Whether playing at St. Joseph's Prep School as an All-City quarterback, playing for the University of Delaware, where he set twenty-one school records, or representing the silver and black of the Raiders, Gannon is known for his consistency, intellect, durability, accuracy, scrambling ability, and field awareness.

This three-time All-Pro quarterback gives full credit to his teammates and supportive family. Even his beautiful wife, Shelley, is considered part of the team. Rich regularly has her grill him on 3 x 5 index cards about play calls, position assignments, and formations. "At the end of the day it's about teamwork and consistency," he says.

And so it is with living the Christian life. It's about teamwork (fellowship in a church) and consistency (daily prayer and Bible reading). Are you working on being a focused and consistent player for the kingdom?

The apostle Paul was a real play-caller, regularly challenging his followers with words of encouragement and commitment. There are times in our lives when we either need to lean on others or we need others to lean upon us.

I'm reminded of a story that helps us appreciate the comfort and sustaining power we can receive from one another. Sadhu Sundar Singh and a companion were traveling through a high pass in the Himalayan Mountains when they came across a body lying in the snow. The man was barely alive. Sadhu told his traveling companion they needed to help the stranger. The companion felt his best chance was to make it on his own.

After his friend left, Sadhu placed the poor traveler upon his shoulders and slowly carried the man onward. The high altitude and snowy conditions caused him to fully exert himself. The heat from his body warmed the victim and gradually restored him to life. The two men struggled together and, leaning upon one another, they kept each other warm and encouraged.

As they neared the end of their destination they came across the frozen, dead body of his first companion. His independent struggle for survival had failed, and he died a lonely, desperate man.

One of the lessons learned from the climbers, and seen every week in any football game, is that no matter how talented any player is, no single individual can carry the whole team. Each player is dependent upon other players to do their job. If everyone has properly prepared himself both physically and mentally, more often than not he will be consistent and focused—and he will be a winner.

As Gannon discovered, initially the role a great leader plays in motivating others to good works is a lonely and unpopular one. His teammates have awarded him the MVPP award for Most Valuable Party Pooper. But that same team is equally proud of the tremendous accomplishments they have recently achieved because they were playing as a team in a consistent and supportive manner.

Look not every man on his own things, but every man also on the things of others.

—Philippians 2:4 KJV

"When you get an athlete, he's got to be motivated, and he's got to be committed. It's like the kamikaze pilot who flew fifty-four missions—he was involved, but he wasn't committed."

—**Lou Holtz,** South Carolina Coach

40

It's About Courage

Most people would define courage as being fearless, having a daring spirit that enables you to meet intimidating challenges head on, having true grit. The word "courage" comes from the French word *coeur*, which means to have heart. Just as the heart lies at the body's core, enabling other parts of the body to function, so courage is central to the Christian, empowering us to manifest other qualities of Christlike character.

To play effectively as a tight end in professional football and to be selected numerous times to represent your conference in the Pro Bowl, you must have courage. To be named as a member of John Madden's "Tough Guy" team, you must be worthy of that title. These are among the highest honors given in the NFL; both were attained by Brent Jones, former tight end of the San Francisco 49ers.

Jones had prepared well during the 1996 preseason. Several nagging injuries were on the mend, and his stamina and strength were outstanding. He regularly worked out with wide receivers Jerry Rice, Terrell Owens, and Mike Singleton to increase his speed and improve his timing.

The 49ers started the season a little slow, as did Jones. He'd had only four passes directed to him, and the offense was looking pretty lethargic. After a loss to Carolina, the 49ers vowed to turn things around, but as they prepared for the Atlanta game, disaster struck. The Sports section headline in the Sunday paper conveyed the bad news: "Jones to Have Shoulder Surgery."

The article read,

> The 49er tight end jinx has struck again. . . . Brent Jones is scheduled for arthroscopic surgery this afternoon to remove an old screw that came loose in his shoulder. Jones partially dislocated his left shoulder in a contact scrimmage Thursday when teammates fell on him.

The shoulder was originally repaired after a separation in high school. Then Jones was in a serious automobile accident, which damaged his neck. In 1995 he was hit hard, and his knee collapsed; he had to be carried off the field only to return a few plays later. Time and time again coaches, reporters, and doctors counted him down and out—finished. Each time God provided a miracle, and Jones displayed the courage that allowed him to return with more passion and persistence than he had before.

Jones went back to his position, making remarkable catches and runs. The 49ers marched on to yet another playoff berth. Fans remember that season with a sense of awe at the determination and courage this man modeled in his life.

However, the biggest battle was off the field. While desire, courage, and guts are admirable qualities in an All-American football player, they can stand in the way of a deep spiritual life. Jones realized that he could only be successful if he placed Jesus Christ at the center of his universe.

> God needed to be in control—not Brent! When I sought to do things on my strength, I usually failed. Things would really get out of whack when I tried to rely on my own wisdom and efforts.
>
> During the course of several injuries and unusual circumstances, I tried to press on thinking that my destiny as an "overcomer" was all I needed to carry the moment. I was wrong. I needed much more. I needed the inner strength that can only come from a relationship with the living God. I needed a Savior to direct and energize my nerve.
>
> When I finally accepted Jesus as my personal Savior and Lord, that's when things really got under control. Proverbs is real clear on where I need to be with the issue of control: "Trust in the Lord with all your heart and lean not on your own understanding; in all your ways acknowledge him, and he will make your paths straight" (3:5–6).

Someone once said, "Courage is not the absence of fear, but the conquest of it." There are at least two types of courage. First, there is the attitude or ability to deal with anything recognized as dangerous, difficult, or painful, instead of running from it. Next is having the boldness to do what one thinks is right. Both definitions fit the profile of Brent Jones.

Sports commentators routinely talked about the special courage he showed on the field. It is truly awesome how he continues to overcome adversity and to stare difficult situations in the face, only to work through them with commitment and integrity.

Jones is not alone among courageous heroes of the faith. I think of people like Joshua as he faced the trials of leadership; Abraham, leaving his homeland to seek out a country for his people and offering his son Isaac as a sacrifice; Gideon, upon attacking the confederate armies of the Midianites and Amalekites; Daniel, being persistent in prayer despite a conspiracy to cast him into the lions' den; Nehemiah, refusing to take no for an answer in rebuilding the temple; Thomas, being willing to die for Jesus; Paul, going to Jerusalem despite his impression that bonds and imprisonment awaited him; and David, challenging the giant Goliath for the right to rule the Promised Land.

Coach George Seifert saw in Jones that same kind of determination, faith, and courage. And like King David, Brent calls upon "the name of the Lord Almighty" (1 Samuel 17:45) to be with him in battles on the line of scrimmage. Because of Jones' physical limitations after his injuries, everyone knows that the glory will go to the Lord.

When you have been protected, encouraged, and strengthened for battle, where does the glory go? Like Brent Jones, do you declare, "The Lord is the strength of my life; of whom then shall I be afraid?" (Psalm 27:1).

You say, "But, Jim, I *am* afraid!" Eddie Rickenbacker, who regularly pushed the envelope of discovery and exploration, said, "Courage is doing what you're afraid to do. There can be no courage unless you're scared."

Every time you approach a new challenge, look to God for the strength and power. Seek his counsel and move forward with courage. You will gain new strength and assurance each time you experience intimidating situations, approach fear head on, stare it down, and do the thing you think you can't. If it is of God, He will provide a way when there seems to be none.

Whether you're an All-Pro football player or a couch-bound fan, your calling is a courageous one—to be a disciple of the living Christ and to help spread the Good News of His love in a hostile environment.

◄▣►

We had too many Marys and not enough Williams.
—Lou Holtz, Former William and Mary Coach,
after a loss to Cincinnati

> "We should've won, but Unitas is a guy who knows what it was to eat potato soup seven days a week as a kid. That's what beat us."
>
> —**Norm Van Brocklin,** Former Rams Coach, after losing to the Colts

41

Mr. Football: Johnny U

During the 1950s and 1960s there was one name that became synonymous with football—Johnny Unitas. During these great growth years of the NFL, Unitas helped carry the sport to the forefront. His work ethic and passion for the game provided his teammates with great inspiration.

Unitas was a self-made man of sorts. His father died early in his life, leaving his family in a desperate situation. Unitas observed his mother's hard work as she returned to night school to further her education while scrubbing floors during the day to make enough money to feed her family.

To help out, the young Unitas shoveled two tons of coal every day after school to help his mom provide for the family. Somehow he squeezed in enough practice time to play varsity football. As hard as he played, no major college was interested in a 5'11", 130-pound quarterback. When hope seemed gone, Unitas began to promote his talents to a few colleges. While the Notre Dame head coach really liked his attitude and style, he told Johnny, "I can't put you out on the field—you'll get killed."

Finally Unitas got a break when the University of Louisville took a chance on him. His college football successes won him a ninth-round draft pick from the Pittsburgh Steelers. Unfortunately, he was cut in his rookie year prior to the beginning of the season. However, rather than quit football,

Unitas decided to keep his skills sharp by playing semi-pro ball at $6 a game. In the "rock 'em, sock 'em" league he once again proved his skill and passion while playing for the Bloomfield Rams.

Finally Don Kellett, the Colts general manager, phoned Unitas and asked him to try out at their May camp. As mentioned earlier, Unitas made the Colts as a backup quarterback. When the starting QB went down with a knee injury, Johnny was inserted into the game. His inexperience was obvious. He fumbled three times and his first throw was greeted with an interception. But failure was something Unitas didn't accept.

While many coaches would have scolded him, Weeb Ewbank consoled and encouraged him. "Don't worry about it," the coach said. "You're my quarterback again next week." Unitas went on to become one of the most successful players in NFL history.

Unitas wrote the playbook on what it takes to win a game in the last two minutes. His style was a mixture of pure genius and unabandoned recklessness. He would run down the field ahead of his runners, blocking anyone in his way. His philosophy was "If you show fear, you've already lost the game."

Not only did he appear in ten Pro Bowls and win League MVP three times, but he also called almost every offensive play from 1958–1971. He masterminded the overtime comeback of the Baltimore Colts in what is arguably the greatest game ever played—the 1958 NFL championship game with the New York Giants. He also threw at least one touchdown pass in each of forty-seven consecutive games, a record that still stands today.

His blue-collar image endeared him to the common laborer. His high-top boots and in-your-face play gave him enormous crowd appeal. One commentator said this about the legendary man: "When the image of the best player to play the game matches the substance—that is Johnny Unitas."

The image of Johnny Unitas is a picture of a determined warrior. His matchless willpower and desire for success helped him become one of the top players to ever lace up a pair of football cleats. It has been said of those who are determined, "Some people dream of success, while others wake up and work hard at it."

Unitas mirrors the determination found in several biblical characters. One such person is a young undersized lad named David. David was not seen to have warrior potential. He was slight of build and seemed to be suited more for watching sheep than slaying the enemy.

And much like the character and determination we see in Johnny U., David worked hard to sell himself to others. He finally convinced his brothers and King Saul to let him have a chance to prove himself and his Lord. With God's help David took on a very tough assignment. The Spirit of God directed his every move as he flung a small rock to triumph over the monstrous Philistine.

David was confident and determined because he knew that with God's help anything is possible. We serve a God who regularly deals with impossible situations. He is the Lord of all possibilities. So it is, my friends: Persevere! Be determined! If a scrawny young boy from a small coal-mining town can become one of the NFL's most distinguished quarterbacks, and if a frail shepherd boy can slay a giant, God can enable you to do far more than you might expect.

A great leader is a person who can evoke the right response in other people.

—Humphrey Mynors

"Character is like a tree and reputation like its shadow. The shadow is what we think of it; the tree is the real thing."

—Abraham Lincoln

Chapter

6

Third
Quarter

The test of success in
life is not what you
achieve, but the
obstacles you overcome
to achieve it!

—Author unknown

> **"B**aseball players are smarter than football players. How often do you see a baseball team penalized for too many men on the field?"
>
> —Jim Bouton

42

Using Our Gifts

In 1936 Slingin' Sammy Baugh was rated "the finest college [football] player in the country." Baugh didn't disappoint the owner of the Washington Redskins, George Preston Marshall, who drafted him as a first-round pick. As a professional player, Baugh went on to set several offensive records, some of which have never been toppled, even by the greats of our day.

Sammy played sixteen seasons with the Redskins. This was before facemasks, high-tech protective gear, and personal trainers. At thirty-eight he was still calling plays and performing at a high level. But after years of battling rushing linemen, Baugh's long, gaunt frame showed ample fatigue and scarring.

In 1952 Baugh and his team lined up against their rivals, the Chicago Cardinals. They were facing a fearsome front four and a hostile Comiskey Park crowd. Time and again Sammy left the protective pocket to complete passes over a frustrated Cardinal defense. Despite a preseason injury to his throwing hand, Baugh's bullet-like passes screamed through the outstretched hands of defensive linemen.

Finally an exasperated Cardinal tackle named Don Joyce had had enough. He ran into the unprotected quarterback and decked him. In a reactive manner, Sammy threw a punch with his legendary right hand. The fight lasted long enough to get both players ejected from the game. That was the last time Sammy Baugh cocked his right arm on a football field. He retired and went on to become a successful assistant coach.

What separated Slingin' Sammy from other passers that came along after him was that he was an original—the real deal! He was to the quarterback position what Henry Ford was to the Model-T. Others had invented the forward pass, but Baugh was the first one to make full use of it. He perfected various formations to take advantage of his accuracy and delivery.

Baugh used his God-given talents and abilities (his natural giftedness) to the fullest. A smart player recognizes his strengths and weaknesses so he can maximize his potential and also allows the coach's instruction to live through him. Sammy was very coachable and teachable. His college and professional coaches spoke confidence and assurance into his life and into his play. They were his mentors, and he duplicated their instruction in his daily workouts and game situations. But Sammy was a team player. He recognized that even though the quarterback was important, so was every member of the team—and they could only win when the entire team pulled together. Each individual used his talent to benefit the greater whole. And they were winners!

In like manner, God wants every Christian to understand his spiritual gifts and use them wisely and in conjunction with others. According to 1 Corinthians 12 and Romans 12, once we accept Christ into our hearts God gives us our spiritual gifts—the methods through which the Holy Spirit ministers to others (1 Corinthians 12:11). Gifts can manifest themselves in a desire and ability to teach, preach, serve, encourage, counsel, sing, administer a program, or other such expressions of service. It is clear that the Holy Spirit empowers the abilities and talents of people so as to speak through them, much in the same way a coach will speak through a good player.

Unlike our football analogy, it would be inaccurate to equate a natural ability with a spiritual gift; the apostle Paul illustrates the difference. He could have used his knowledge of philosophy, language, and literature to write and speak great messages. Instead, he said, "I did not come with superiority of speech or of wisdom, proclaiming to you the testimony of God. For I determined to know nothing among you except Jesus Christ, and Him crucified" (1 Corinthians 2:1–2 NASB).

We are encouraged in Scripture not to sit on our spiritual gifts; we *must* use them. Peter says this concerning our abilities:

As each one has received a special gift, employ it in serving one another, as good stewards of the manifold grace of God. Whoever speaks, let him speak, as it were, the utterances of God; whoever serves, let him do so as by the strength which God supplies; so that in all things God may be glorified through Jesus Christ. (1 Peter 4:10–11 NASB)

But to each one is given the manifestation of the Spirit for the common good.

—1 Corinthians 12:7 NASB

> "Playing cornerback is like being on an island—people can see you but they can't help you."
>
> —Eddie Lewis

43

Overcoming Fear

Today there is a great deal of talk about fear. Left in the background of our consciousness are the memories of our concern for how we would survive Y2K or the outbreak of AIDS. Now our fears have settled upon the problems associated with terrorism and disease. Daily we pick up newspapers and read about the threat of bombings, the hijacking of planes, and violence in far-away places. There is no doubt we live in fearful times.

From meeting many NFL players, I can attest to the fact that most of these guys are fearless people. The size and speed of modern-day players create many opportunities whereby a player could get hurt. Despite the evolution of modern equipment, many players still lose teeth, crack their nose, receive a concussion, break bones, and occasionally suffer a crippling hit that paralyzes them.

If fear exists in the NFL, it will first be seen among those small, fleet-of-foot cornerbacks that often attempt to take on players weighing a hundred pounds more than they do. The three basic defenses (zone, man-to-man, and prevent) present different problems and risk to the cornerbacks.

The zone defense relies on the cornerbacks taking a specific side of the field, leaving the safeties to cover the middle. Most often the receivers and halfbacks have built up a pretty good head of steam before they reach the corners' area. This is when some of the most violent collisions occur. In man-to-man coverage, the back is usually bumping the opponent at the line of scrimmage, then running with him, matching the receivers' direction and speed. Finally, the prevent defense is often used late in the second or fourth quarter when additional cornerbacks are placed in the game in order to prevent the bomb.

"Cornerbacks have the toughest job on the field. I don't envy them for a minute. I don't miss being over there. I like being able to sleep the night before a game" (Roy Green, Former Cardinal Cornerback-Turned-Receiver).

Al Davis, who was a great coach and commissioner of the AFL and who is now the owner of the three-time world champion Oakland Raiders, has this to say about cornerbacks: "The most important players on a football team are the cornerbacks. You start with great cornerbacks, then you build the rest of your team."

One of the best corners to ever play the game was the late Los Angeles Ram Dick "Night Train" Lane. Lane was a punishing tackler with quick reflexes, and as a rookie he had fourteen interceptions, which is still the NFL record. "At cornerback," Lane often said, "you're going to get beat, but you've got to have a sense of recovery."

Passive or timid players are at risk because they allow the action to come to them instead of being proactive in their assignment. All-Pro safety/cornerback Rod Woodson says, "If you want to be the best cornerback, you have to play like a linebacker. You have to take on pulling guards and tackles, and you must hit tight ends and running backs." Woodson and other great cornerbacks take the position that fear is something they must control and put out of their mind. They have learned that if fear controls them, they will not be able to perform to their capabilities.

It's probably good to provide a word of caution to younger players. A commonsense respect and appreciation for your talents and abilities goes a long way in remaining injury-free. There is no place for crazy players who simply run around crashing into people. The reason undersized cornerbacks last in the NFL is that they are highly trained and skilled in knowing how to take and give a hit.

God has indicated that the last days for humankind will be full of problems that could undermine our spiritual vitality if we allow them to. Anxiety is a joy-robber that will affect our vibrant witness and worship of God.

What is it that you fear today?

- trepidation about the loss of security?
- stress about a long journey you are about to take?
- worry about something threatening a personal relationship?
- concern about loved ones?
- anxiety about the future and its implications for the stock market?
- fear about a pending medical exam/report that might bring bad news?

Lloyd Ogilvie, in his book *Twelve Steps to Living Without Fear*, notes that fear has reached epidemic proportions in America. It's contagious: We become infected with it and pass it on to others. Like a disease, fear saps our energy and pervades our families, even our churches.

The Bible has much to say about fear. The heartening challenge "Fear not" appears 366 times in Scripture, once for each day of the year. When God directs us to *fear not*, He wants us to trust and obey Him while being confident of His control over every situation.

In the Old Testament we find a courageous man who often confronted his fears. As a young lad he stood up to a lion, a bear, and a giant. Yet we often read about his working through his worries as he talked with God. King David had his weak times just like you and me. However, despite stressful situations, he ultimately sought the comfort of the living God.

Jesus asked His disciples during a particularly fearful time on a windy sea, "Why are you so afraid? Do you still have no faith?" (Mark 4:40). Let's work on our trust and obedience to an all-powerful God. Attack fear before it attacks you.

We were tipping off our plays. Whenever we broke from the huddle, three backs were laughing and one was pale as a ghost.
—*John Breen, Former Oilers General Manager*

"Merlin Olsen is very big, very strong, has great speed and great agility, is a very smart ballplayer, gives at least 110 percent on every play, and those are his weak points."

—Jerry Kramer

44

A Superstar Athlete

The average NFL player lasts about three and a half years before he retires to regular life. A few players might even make it to seven years. As you search the annals of football history, most of the athletes who have lasted beyond ten years usually begin to show a decline in performance near the end of their career.

Even the most dedicated athlete will become slower and more cautious as he ages. The rigor of mini-camps, training camp, off-season conditioning, and a regular season schedule places the athlete and his family under unique testing.

Many have called Jerry Rice the greatest player to ever play football. His coaches and teammates will unanimously agree he is the hardest-working man in the game. Rice continues to amaze the football world with his endurance, confidence, perseverance, ability, spirit, and, most of all, his work ethic.

I happened to be on the field both times Rice was hurt. The injury and the re-injury to his knee seemed to be career-ending. After all, how could he keep playing? *Why* would he keep on playing? What is the point of trying to set even more records when he practically owns the record book for a receiver?

When the San Francisco 49ers hit the salary cap wall at the beginning of

162

the 2001 season, Rice became expendable. While the Niners loved him, they no longer could afford to carry an aging sixteen-year veteran. We all thought, *Well, it's finally over.* That is, everyone but Rice. After negotiations with the Oakland Raiders, he once again took the field to continue his quest of setting more records and showing the world that his work ethic and passion for the game were still perking along at a youthful pace.

I know of no other athlete who, prior to entering the 2002 season, holds fourteen NFL records and sixteen club records, has twice been named NFL Player of the Year (1987, 1990), has been to thirteen Pro Bowls, and has 20,386 receiving yards with 185 receiving touchdowns. This amazing athlete also owns *four* Super Bowl rings and has set several additional records while competing in that ultimate contest.

Most players are fortunate to have one page of historical and personal information in their team's media guide. Not so with Mr. Fantastic—his credentials and history take a full six pages. To fully appreciate this man, one needs to review just a few of the NFL records he has set. What is it that allows Jerry Rice to continue to excel? It would take more pages than I've got to elucidate the various aspects of his personality, his commitment, his pride, his physical conditioning, his persona, and his character.

The thing I notice most is his work ethic. When Rice came across the Bay and joined the Oakland Raiders, he established a new "Jerry Standard." Despite two-a-day workouts, hot temperatures, pursuing media, and the need to get some rest, he was always the first one on the practice field.

While other players were sitting in the shade of the training facility— getting taped up, quaffing one more power drink, reading the newspaper, telling jokes—Rice was on a corner of the field practicing moves and running patterns by himself. His eyes were focused on his footwork and not the swarming media. His focus was riveted to wrapping his hands around the ball.

While executing warm-up plays with the offense, Jerry Rice and Tim Brown were the only two to run beyond the expected thirty-yard route all the way into the end zone. This was not just on an occasional play, but every single time they touched the ball.

The avid fan might think perfection is somehow embodied in the person of Jerry Rice. Whether or not he is the greatest man to ever play the game will be determined over a view of history by those capable of judging his contribution. One thing I do know for sure is that he isn't perfect. By his own admission, he works hard at his sport because he knows that there are weaknesses in his game.

God's Word helps us understand how our Lord defines perfection. The parable of the rich young ruler comes to mind:

> Now a man came up to Jesus and asked, "Teacher, what good thing must I do to get eternal life?"
>
> "Why do you ask me about what is good?" Jesus replied. "There is only One who is good. If you want to enter life, obey the commandments."
>
> "Which ones?" the man inquired.
>
> Jesus responded, "Do not murder, do not commit adultery, do not steal, do not give false testimony, honor your father and mother, and love your neighbor as yourself."
>
> "All these I have kept," the young man said. "What do I still lack?"
>
> Jesus answered, "If you want to be perfect, go, sell your possessions and give to the poor, and you will have treasure in heaven. Then come, follow me."
>
> When the young man heard this, he went away sad, because he had great wealth. Then Jesus said to his disciples, "I tell you the truth, it is hard for a rich man to enter the kingdom of heaven.... It is easier for a camel to go through the eye of a needle." (Matthew 19:16–24)

The rich young ruler was thinking in terms of righteousness by works; Jesus had to correct this misunderstanding first before answering his question more fully. Jesus directs the man's attention to the fact that there is only One who is good and perfect—God himself: "Under the old system, even the high priests were weak and sinful men who could not keep from doing wrong, but later God appointed by his oath his Son who is perfect forever" (Hebrews 7:28 TLB).

The Bible teaches that unless we accept Christ as our Savior we cannot enter the kingdom of heaven. It isn't about works, or performance, or pride, or who we know, or how many resources we have, or if we make it to the Hall of Fame. No, God's Word is clear: The gift of eternal life is provided by grace—God's unmerited favor.

No matter how righteous or perfect we think we might be, all of us have failed. We all deserve permanent separation from a holy and righteous God, but He provided a sacrifice—a perfect sacrifice—in the form of His Son. He never sinned, or in football terms, never missed a pass. He took the burden of our sin to the cross that we might be free to have a personal relationship with God. "For by that one offering he made forever perfect in the sight of God all those whom he is making holy" (Hebrews 10:14 TLB).

We must first accept that relationship and be willing to turn from our sinful past. When we do, we can expect to receive the most perfect gift of all. Because of Christ, God sees us as perfect:

> And it was right and proper that God, who made everything for his own glory, should allow Jesus to suffer, for in doing this he was bringing vast multitudes of God's people to heaven; for his suffering made Jesus a perfect Leader, one fit to bring them into their salvation. (Hebrews 2:10 TLB)

But whatever is good and perfect comes to us from God, the Creator of all light, and he shines forever without change or shadow.

—James 1:17 TLB

"I didn't see the ball. I barely saw the blur."

—**Lester Hayes,** Former Raider Cornerback,
on a John Elway pass

45

An Odd Season

I n the summer of 2001 players swarmed to various football training camp facilities across the nation, expecting the same old thing. Anticipation ran high as they became accustomed to the two-a-day drills associated with preparing for a rigorous season. No one expected 2001 to be defined by numerous peculiar occurrences that would impact every player's future.

In the middle of the year one wondered if this strange NFL season could become any more bizarre before experiencing the final game, the Super Bowl, slated for February instead of January.

- A player dies during training camp from heat stroke.
- A few players are suspended for the season because of drug use.
- A game is canceled just minutes before kickoff in front of a national television audience, and a city is embarrassed, because their artificial turf was not ready for play.
- College officials replaced striking NFL referees for the first few regular season games.
- A group of fans sue a team over season tickets.
- More rookie quarterbacks take starting jobs than in any other season.
- Thirteen teams start new quarterbacks.

- The All-Pro quarterback who led his team to a Super Bowl victory the previous season was released and is playing for another team.
- The season was put on hold for ten days while our nation grieved the loss of thousands of victims associated with the terrorist attacks.
- New security policies and policing of what can be taken to a game are strictly enforced.
- NFL team training and office facilities are placed under armed security.
- In the last week of regular play eight teams still have a shot to lock up a playoff berth.
- The Oakland Raiders, who looked unstoppable in midseason, lose their last three games in the last seconds by an average margin of three points.
- Fans actually appreciate and sing the national anthem at games.
- Prayer and reverent attitudes have returned to many campuses and halftime programs.

Change is inevitable! There are times in our lives and in the course of a season that drastic alterations have to occur so we can adapt to the situation.

To be successful in playing the position of quarterback you need to have a strong arm, be a team leader, have quick reflexes, be able to withstand stress and conflict, be durable, have quick feet, and be an intelligent person. But there's one more thing he absolutely must have—a loud voice! All the offensive players on the field must be able to hear their field general bark out orders that reveal the formation, snap count, and any audible that might change the play. If players can't hear the commands, they will jump offside, become confused, or be in the wrong place at the wrong time.

In September 1980, Steve DeBerg of the San Francisco 49ers met all of the qualifications associated with being a top NFL quarterback. That is, until he contracted laryngitis—DeBerg lost his voice while leading the 49ers to an upset victory over the New Orleans Saints in the opening game of the season. The week after San Francisco's win, his voice got worse instead of better. During practice, no one could hear him call signals—his voice was barely audible. Since he was the 49ers first-string QB, replacing him before the team's next game against the St. Louis Cardinals was out of the question.

Forty-niner officials got permission from the NFL to wire DeBerg's helmet with a specially built microphone that would amplify the quarterback's voice and permit him to "broadcast" signals to his teammates on the field. The microphone worked like magic for DeBerg, who completed twenty-five of forty-three passes for three TDs and 266 yards as he led the 49ers to a 24–21 victory over the Cardinals.

After September 11, 2001, adapting to change has become a routine part of our daily existence. We are now a country where personal freedoms and liberties have been modified so that security issues can be addressed more effectively. We once believed that our government and financial structures were invincible to any sort of threat. Today we have changed our view on how we go about governing this great nation and how we maintain our freedom and security.

The pace at which we live our lives speaks of a hurried sickness found among most Americans. The computer industry is an example of how current technology today will not be current tomorrow. Just in the past few years this author went from a laptop that had a two-megabyte hard drive to a sixteen-gigabyte one that can instantly hook me up with information sources all over the world. We live in a fast-paced, ever-changing world.

Values and character are constantly being challenged. What we blushed at only a few years ago is now seen as common language and action. Those unmentionables are now freely discussed on television and radio talk shows. Like the pendulum on a grandfather clock, social standards vacillate back and forth.

With all the variability and adaptation, it's good to know that there are some things that will never change. As believers we can count on it:

"I the Lord do not change. So you, O descendants of Jacob, are not destroyed." (Malachi 3:6 NASB)

For I am convinced that neither death nor life, neither angels nor demons, neither the present nor the future, nor any powers, neither height nor depth, nor anything else in all creation, will be able to separate us from the love of God that is in Christ Jesus our Lord. (Romans 8:38–39)

The grass withers and the flowers fall, but the word of our God stands forever. (Isaiah 40:8)

But as for you, continue in what you have learned and have become convinced of, because you know those from whom you learned it, and how from infancy you have known the holy Scriptures, which are able to make you wise for salvation through faith in Christ Jesus. All Scripture is God-breathed and is useful for teaching, rebuking, correcting and training in righteousness, so that the man of God may be thoroughly equipped for every good work. (2 Timothy 3:14–17)

He who is the Glory of Israel does not lie or change his mind; for he is not a man, that he should change his mind. (1 Samuel 15:29)

The plans of the Lord stand firm forever, the purposes of his heart through all generations. (Psalm 33:11)

And we know that in all things God works for the good of those who love him, who have been called according to his purpose. (Romans 8:28)

Dear friend, please know that the only thing you can really count on is a relationship with God. Whether you're in business, a homemaker, a laborer, the president of the United States, or an NFL player, change will occur. If you allow your mood and attitude to be regulated by a lack of stability and consistency in your life, you open yourself up to major disappointment and an unfulfilled life.

The most together players I know recognize this and seek the stability in life that can only come through a personal relationship with the living God.

Many are the plans in a man's heart,
but it is the Lord's purpose that prevails.

—*Proverbs 19:21*

"I haven't seen a new play since I was in high school."

—Red Grange

46

The Playbook

Today's prototype quarterback can no longer be just a great athlete; he must also be a student of the game and have an excellent memory. In order to help slow down high-powered, blitzing defenses, many NFL teams have gone to complicated motion plays that produce numerous options for the quarterback.

Some teams now have offensive playbooks that boast of 150–170 different plays! In addition to worrying about four angry defensive linemen trying to tear his head off and being preoccupied with a blitzing linebacker or two, the modern quarterback must quickly determine where each of his three to five receivers will be at any point in time during the play. If his primary receiver is not open, he must check off to his secondary and tertiary receivers, hoping one of them will break free of the coverage.

Even though players who reach the pro level are already familiar with the basics found in all team playbooks, most NFL teams spend a lot of time in classroom situations, reviewing all the possibilities that exist. In addition to the chalk talks, diagrams, films, videos, and Polaroids, today's classrooms have sophisticated computers that allow the players to see field situations in several dimensions.

Some teams actually utilize a "virtual reality stage" to help key players better anticipate the tendencies of the opponent prior to actually meeting them on the field. And some teams even have very large mainframes that allow a quarterback sitting in a remote room to access a specific play, formation, or replay for every team in the NFL. Welcome to the world of technology.

However, nothing can replace the intelligence and abilities of a great quarterback. Most coaches would say that Bernie Kosar, who played for the Cleveland Browns and the Dallas Cowboys, was one of the quickest studies in the game. Kosar was released by the Browns after the 1993 season began; a week earlier Cowboy Troy Aikman had suffered a hamstring pull that sidelined him, so Dallas grabbed Kosar. In three days' time, he learned sixty-seven Cowboy offensive plays. Offensive coordinator Norv Turner was impressed: "Kosar learned the nuts and bolts of our attack in a very short time. His numbers for the first game: thirteen completions in twenty-one attempts for 199 yards with no interceptions and a great touchdown pass to Jay Orvacek."

Despite the ability and collegiate experience of most rookie quarterbacks, there are precious few who can come into the NFL and take over the reins immediately. A dedicated player will study and analyze for years before his reactions to a set of signals become automatic.

Most folks spend about an hour a day listening to the radio, watching television, or reading a newspaper to get caught up on the news. Many attend seminars, retreats, conferences, and workshops to find more efficient and effective ways to complete a task. We study these resources to try to find meaning in life, or to learn how to respond to difficulty, or to discover how to be more successful in our chosen occupation.

While all these things will help educate and build self-esteem, none can offer answers to some of the most basic questions in life. I've occasionally visited with people in the hospital who are fighting for their last breath. No one has ever told me they wish they had put in one more day of work at the office. No one has ever said they needed to see one more touchdown play from their favorite quarterback. Yet many have asked me if there truly is a heaven. They also ask if God loves them enough to save them from eternal damnation. With tears in their eyes they tell me that their faith in God and time with their family are the only true values in life.

The playbook for life is the Holy Bible. The truths contained in the sixty-six books that comprise it have not changed in thousands of years; the message contained in the Good Book provides answers to the issues challenging us at home, in our place of employment, with our neighbors, and at school. The information in God's Word is knowledge and wisdom that informs, transforms, conforms, and reforms our very souls.

The Bible is a valuable resource to tell us about the past, the present, and the future. Like looking at an NFL playbook, we will be able to anticipate the very moves that will take place in our society and in our world. God's Word renews our mind and renovates our spirit: "Do not conform any longer to the pattern of this world, but be transformed by the renewing of your mind. Then you will be able to test and approve what God's will is—his good, pleasing and perfect will" (Romans 12:2).

Take the opportunity to read a chapter a day. If at the end of a year the Bible hasn't transformed your life, I will be surprised.

How can a young man keep his way pure? By living according to your Word.

—*Psalm 119:9*

> **"B**ill Walsh's system could make me a good quarterback, and I can't even throw the ball in the ocean from the beach."
>
> —Jerry Glanville, Television Analyst

47

The West Coast Offense

The West Coast Offense has become extremely popular with many offensive coordinators. Operated correctly, it is very difficult to stop. The fast-hitting passing attack and a slash-and-slam running game create a lot of movement and surprise potential.

Some say the original West Coast Offense was a product of Oakland Raider Al Davis or San Diego Charger Sid Gilman, both of whom were very pass-oriented. Others claim that it was the by-product of "the Genius"—Coach Bill Walsh, who guided the 49ers to several Super Bowl victories.

The West Coast Offense has lots of motion from the backs and receivers; repeated short passes allow gifted runners to break tackles in the open field. There is a great deal of zone blocking, and the running backs operate out of single-back or "I" formations.

The key to this recently developed offense is deception. One coach said, "It's all about fooling your opponent and keeping him off balance." The quick-hitting offense helps reduce the effectiveness of mobile and agile linebackers who like to blitz. By the time they get to the quarterback, he has already released the ball. In a West Coast Offense, instead of doing a five- or seven-step drop, the wary QB moves three steps back and immediately hits a receiver.

Most coaches will agree that three things are needed to make this offense work:

(1) Players must be smart and listen carefully to each play call. The average West Coast Offense may have more than one hundred and fifty plays that involve various men in motion off a basic formation. The players must keep track of where their opponents are, remember the snap count, and be able to move into a new position at the proper time.

(2) A team must be patient and disciplined to allow the time necessary for all the motion men to do their thing while not false-starting or having two men move simultaneously. It requires that the coach communicate the new play to the quarterback quickly so that he has enough time after breaking the huddle to set his teammates in motion.

(3) Receivers must be fast and precise in their patterns—it's all about timing. With an accurate quarterback and a receiver who runs perfect routes, a quick slant is almost unstoppable. If a team needs five yards, a QB can make a bullet-like throw, low and away from the defender, allowing only his receiver to have a good shot at catching it.

Many of today's NFL coaches who studied under Walsh have taken their initial concepts of his system and have modified their play selection to take advantage of the individual skills and abilities of selected key players. An explosive running attack complements the short passing game. The big and powerful back that lumbers through the line is not as effective as a quicker moving back that can also be used as a receiver.

Too much time in the pocket allows the onrushing defensive players an opportunity to sack the quarterback. In an era when so many starting QBs have been seriously injured, thereby placing the effectiveness of the offense in jeopardy, it is almost a necessity that coaches develop schemes that allow the ball to be delivered to another player within seconds.

To make the West Coast Offense work, you need a wily and seasoned veteran who can see a great deal of the field of play, who carefully selects the most open receiver, who is alert and accurate in his throws. Today there is less of a requirement for the gunner who can whip the ball seventy yards down the field—he is of less value than a ball-control, quick-thinking, accurate passer who is able to respond to more situations.

Some time ago I remember reading a book titled *The Controlled Spirit Temperament*, which has long disappeared from my library shelves (along with scores of others loaned out and never returned). What I remember of the book deals with how we need to work at being under control. Our natural, worldly flesh suggests, "If it feels good, do it." However, once we receive Christ into our lives we are filled with a Spirit that is not of this earth. To some this will sound mystical, yet God intended it to be very understandable: "I will pour out my Spirit on all people" (Joel 2:28; Acts 2:17). The apostle Peter at Pentecost reminded his listeners that they would receive "the gift of the Holy Spirit" if they repented and were baptized (Acts 2:37–39).

I know I need help calling the plays in my life. I appreciate knowing that the ultimate Coach and Counselor runs my West Coast Offense. He can run yours too—just ask God to come into your heart and take over your life. He will help guide you in all your decisions.

◀▥▶

These things God has revealed to us through the Spirit.
—*1 Corinthians 2:10* NRSV

48

A Father's Encouragement

Bob Richards, the former pole vault champion, shares a moving story about a skinny young boy who loved football with all his heart. Practice after practice, the boy eagerly gave everything he had to playing the game. But being half the size of the other lads, he got absolutely nowhere. At all the games this hopeful athlete sat on the bench and hardly ever played.

The teenager lived with his father, just the two of them, and they had a special relationship. Even though the son was a bench jockey, his father was always in the stands cheering, never missing a game. The young man was still the smallest in his class when he entered high school.

The father continued to support, but he also made it very clear that his son did not have to play football if he didn't want to. However, the young man loved the game and decided to hang in there. He was determined to do his best at every practice; perhaps he'd get to play when he became a senior. All through high school he never missed a practice or a game, remaining a benchwarmer all four years. His faithful father remained in the stands, always with words of encouragement.

When the young man went to college, he decided to try out for the football team as a walk-on. Everyone was sure he could never make the cut, but he did. The coach admitted that he kept him on the roster because he always put his heart and soul into every practice, and at the same time modeled for his teammates the spirit and hustle they badly needed. The news that he survived the final cut thrilled the young player so much that he rushed to the nearest phone and called his father. His father shared his excitement, and the son sent him season tickets.

As in high school, the persistent young athlete never missed a practice during his four years at college, but he never played in a game. It was now near the end of his senior football season, and as he trotted onto the practice field shortly before a big playoff game, the coach met him with a telegram. The young man read the message and became deathly silent. Swallowing hard, he mumbled to the coach, "My father died this morning. Is it all right if I miss practice today?" The coach put his arm gently around his shoulders and said, "Take the rest of the week off, son. And don't even plan to come back for the game on Saturday."

Saturday arrived, and the game was not going well. In the third quarter, when the team was ten points behind, a silent young man quietly slipped into the empty locker room and put on his football gear. As he ran onto the sidelines, the coach and his players were astonished to see their faithful teammate back so soon.

"Coach, please let me play. I've just got to play today," said the young man. The coach pretended not to hear him; there was no way he wanted his worst player in this close playoff game. But the young man persisted, and finally, feeling sorry for the kid, the coach gave in. "All right," he said. "You can go in." Before long, the coach, the players, and everyone in the stands couldn't believe their eyes.

The little unknown player, who had never played in a sanctioned game, was doing everything right. He ran, passed, blocked, and tackled like a star, and his team began to triumph—the score was soon tied. In the closing seconds of the game, the young man intercepted a pass and ran it back for the winning touchdown.

The fans broke loose, his teammates hoisted him onto their shoulders—such cheering you've never heard. Finally, after the stands had emptied and the team had showered and left the locker room, the coach noticed the young man sitting quietly alone in the corner. The coach came to him and said, "Kid, I can't believe it. You were fantastic! Tell me, what got into you? How did you do it?" The young man looked at the coach, with tears in his eyes, and said, "Well, you knew my dad died, but did you know that he was blind?" He swallowed hard and forced a smile. "Dad came to all my games, but today was the first time he could see me play, and I wanted to show him I could do it!"

Like this athlete's father, God is always there cheering for us, always reminding us to go on. He's even offering us His hand, for He knows what is best and is willing to give us what we need and not simply what we want. God has never missed a single game. What a joy to know that life is meaningful if lived for the highest goal. Live for HIM; He's watching and helping us in the game of life!

Let us outdo each other in being helpful and kind to each other and in doing good.

—Hebrews 10:24 TLB

49

Paradox

Football, like most sports, has many components that seem paradoxical. Why is it that the smallest guy on the field is often expected to be the last defense against a raging bull-like running back? Did you ever stop to consider that often players are compensated for what they did in the past and not necessarily how they will perform in the future?

Here's a real paradox: A little rural community in Pine Village, Indiana, was once a national power in the sport of professional football.

In the late 1890s, Clinton Beckett, the principal of the small Pine Village School and a high school teacher, introduced the sport of football to the Villagers. Two teams were formed, one from the high school students and one from former students and twenty-year-olds who then competed for county bragging rights. This tradition continued for almost twenty years.

Some wise entrepreneurs got into the mix and began to buy and sell the rights to utilize some of the former high school players so they could create an independent league. Part-time coaches joined the part-time players on weekends to play a game or two. It is reported that they offered not much more than an opportunity for "drinking and rowdyism." The spectators on the sidelines were more likely to get injured (in a brawl) than the ill-equipped players on the field.

The coaches built a traveling team that began to play some of the other upstart independent teams. Some accounts indicate that the "renegade Pine Village team was made up of sizable players that played very rough." Newspaper accounts confirm that some teams would refuse to play Pine Village because of their fierce reputation.

For one game the Mickey Athletic Club of Indianapolis came to play Pine Village. They left town almost as quickly as they came after losing by a score of 111–0. This game gave way to more professional contests against teams made up of former college players coached by the famous Knute Rockne and others who took the game much more seriously than Pine Village.

Pine Village played thirteen games for the season, scoring 259 points to their opponents' 35 and claiming both the Indiana State Championship and the World Championship. Many of their players were the "who's who" of football stars from major colleges.

Time passed, and World War I took many able-bodied men away from football to fight America's enemies. When players returned, Pine Village, Indiana, had discovered basketball. Many of the outstanding players were getting too old to play, and it was time to focus on making a living. However, with their history, a small rural community made up of tough twenty-year-olds helped usher in the interest in this new sport that ultimately created the National Football League.

According to Scripture, except for Jesus Christ, King Solomon was the wisest man ever to live. In the book of Ecclesiastes (3:1), Solomon points out that everything has its time: "To everything there is a season, a time for every purpose under heaven" (NKJV). And everything, including football, will eventually come to an end, because the end of time is coming.

What are your thoughts regarding the end of this age? Are you ready? Ponder this anonymous message found in an email:

> We have taller buildings, but shorter tempers; wider freeways, but narrower viewpoints; we spend more, but have less; we buy more, but enjoy it less.
>
> We have bigger houses and smaller families; more conveniences, but less time; we have more degrees, but less common sense; more knowledge, but less judgment; more experts, but more problems; more medicine, but less wellness.
>
> We spend too recklessly, laugh too little, drive too fast, get too angry

too quickly, stay up too late, get up too tired, read too little, watch TV too much, and pray too seldom.

We have multiplied our possessions, but reduced our values. We talk too much, love too seldom, and lie too often.

We've learned how to make a living, but not a life; we've added years to life, but not life to years.

We've been all the way to the moon and back, but have trouble crossing the street to meet the new neighbor.

We've conquered outer space, but not inner space; we've done larger things, but not better things.

We've cleaned up the air, but polluted the soul.

We've split the atom, but not our prejudice.

We write more, but learn less; plan more, but accomplish less.

We've learned to rush, but not to wait; we have higher incomes, but lower morals; more food, but less appeasement; more acquaintances, but fewer friends; more effort, but less success.

We build more computers to hold more information, to produce more copies than ever, but have less communication; we've become long on quantity, but short on quality.

These are the times of fast foods and slow digestion; tall men and short character; steep profits and shallow relationships.

These are the times of world peace, but domestic warfare; more leisure and less fun; more kinds of food, but less nutrition.

These are days of two incomes, but more divorce; of fancier houses, but broken homes.

These are days of quick trips, disposable diapers, throwaway morality, one-night stands, and pills that do everything from cheer, to quiet, to kill.

It is a time when there is much in the show window and nothing in the stockroom.

Indeed, it's all sad but true.

[Let us not forsake] the assembling of ourselves together, as is the manner of some.

—Hebrews 10:25 NKJV

Chapter

Fourth Quarter

Leadership is a matter of having people look at you and gain confidence, seeing how you react. If you're in control, they're in control.

—Tom Landry

> "We could triple-team [Steve Largent] for that matter. But why embarrass three guys at once?"
>
> —**Darryl Rogers**, Former Lions Coach

50

Finishing Strong

In observing good coaches it's common to hear them admonish their players: "Finish strong!" Those who ultimately find their way to the Pro Bowl are players who know how to finish the play; they are committed to doing what is required until the whistle blows, and they know how to complete the task.

All-Pro receiver Jerry Rice has set the standard for future wideouts. To watch him practice is to watch a master craftsman at work. When Rice runs a pattern, he doesn't quit until he is standing in the end zone. While most receivers break off their pattern when the coach blows the whistle, he continues running until he has exhausted the defensive back or hit the goal line. Then he hustles back to the huddle for his next mission.

It matters not that this takes a few extra seconds away from the next play—Rice is determined to finish strong each time. The additional yardage he puts on during the course of a two-a-day training camp strengthens his legs, improves his stamina, and helps develop an attitude of commitment. Rice has consistently led the league in the YAC (Yards After Catch) category because he's committed to not giving up after he's caught the ball.

Whether playing for a Super Bowl ring or competing in the final game of a relatively unsuccessful season, Rice's philosophy is the same: He plans on finishing strong! He is focused on every game despite the fact that it may not have significance in regard to postseason play.

"If a journeyman cornerback watches Jerry Rice on film, all he can do when the lights go up is ask for help" (Ahmad Rashad, Former Viking Receiver).

The words "finish strong" are wise counsel not only for a great athlete but also for all of us with a weary heart. Specifically, we need to keep focused upon the victory that is ours through a personal, trusting relationship with Jesus Christ. The apostle Paul had numerous imprisonments, as well as other difficulties that would have worn down most people. His strong determination allowed him to pen these words provided by the Holy Spirit: "I count all things to be loss in view of the surpassing value of knowing Christ Jesus my Lord, for whom I have suffered the loss of all things, and count them but rubbish in order that I may gain Christ" (Philippians 3:8 NASB).

No amount of punishment, pressure, doubt, fear, or disbelief was going to take away Paul's victorious moments that would ultimately become steps to success. Paul knew that if he focused upon God instead of his circumstances, he would succeed in being an effective witness for Jesus. How else could a man who had been beaten, left for dead, abandoned, and imprisoned write these words, which we have already examined: "Be anxious for nothing, but in everything by prayer and supplication with thanksgiving let your requests be made known to God. And the peace of God, which surpasses all comprehension, shall guard your hearts and your minds in Christ Jesus" (Philippians 4:6–7 NASB).

My friend, the answer is as simple as kicking an extra point: Paul had a fixed focus on his loving, gracious Savior—the attitude of his heart was set on the Lord. He never forgot the lessons learned along the Damascus Road, where he felt God's unconditional love. Paul was committed to the course laid out before him; his target was identified and his purpose resolute.

Our attitude shapes the way we view life. Are you feeling like you want to quit or slow down? Perhaps you need to more precisely define your goals and commitments. Maybe your focus is on your circumstances rather than your Savior. Don't doubt, don't waver, don't change course: "Finish Strong!"

When you have a size-fourteen shoe, you land on your feet most of the time.

—Sam Wyche, Fired Bengals Coach,
on receiving the Tampa Bay job

51

Interceptions Don't Need to Be Fatal

When an NFL quarterback drops back to pass, the one thing he doesn't want to do is throw an interception. Unfortunately, in the heat of the battle, what a quarterback wants and what can happen to the misguided pigskin may be two different things.

Take the case of quarterback Jim Hardy of the old Chicago Cardinals. On September 24, 1950, against the Philadelphia Eagles, Jim's performance was less than spectacular: He attempted thirty-nine passes and was intercepted a record eight times in a single game!

Quarterback/placekicker George Blanda was also famous for chucking the football into the wrong places. In 1962, while playing for the Houston Oilers, Blanda tossed forty-two interceptions in one season. He is the NFL leader in career interceptions with a total of 277, but he is also a record holder in several positive areas. His philosophy was "Put the thing in the air—you have a 50 percent chance that something good can happen."

Then there are the accurate quarterbacks like Johnny Unitas, Bart Starr, Joe Montana, Steve Young, Troy Aikman, Kurt Warner, and Rich Gannon—precise in their passing and not willing to just chuck the ball into the air and hope for "good things to happen." As an example, from 1964 through 1965

Bart Starr of the Packers set an NFL record by attempting 294 passes in a row without a single interception.

Today's skilled quarterbacks, operating in the "lower risk" West Coast Offense, often find a better ratio of touchdowns to interceptions. In this offensive scheme, most QBs are attempting high-percentage passes in the five-to-fifteen-yard range. The three-step drop and quick release often help them to complete throws before the defensive backs have a chance to react.

The possibility of an interception should not deter a quarterback from throwing the ball. An experienced QB will make decisions and react accordingly. If the possibility of an interception seems low to moderate, given the possibility for gain, they will throw the ball. Nothing ventured, nothing gained.

One of my favorite quotes on risk taking comes from the great Teddy Roosevelt: "Far better is it to dare mighty things, to win glorious triumphs even though checkered by failure, than to rank with those poor spirits who neither enjoy nor suffer much because they live in the gray twilight that knows neither victory nor defeat."

To be a successful passer you need to constantly refine and perfect your skills while taking some risks. The discipline of working on being extremely accurate is of utmost importance. The quarterback's passing drills involve frequent opportunities to "thread the needle" by throwing the pigskin into very tight spots.

So it is with being a disciple: It's about practice and commitment. Jesus is perpetually involved in perfecting us, the saints, for the work of ministry; He uses our circumstances in the process. You and I, as disciples, are to make other disciples who can in turn reproduce themselves. Discipleship is apprenticeship—it is the process of sharing, encouraging, modeling, teaching, listening, and serving.

Great quarterbacks aren't born into the position. Success happens because a person is devoted to a great deal of hard work and through his mentors is refined and perfected. In the case of the quarterback his coaches will help shape and mold the young man into a player.

Ken Carpenter, editor for *Spirit of Revival* magazine, understands that discipleship is exactly what God's Word teaches us about the persistence and patience it takes to be a mature Christian. He states: "Discipleship is a process. God's desire is to etch into our lives the imprint of His Son, Jesus. He is responsible for the construction process of making us like Christ. But He needs yielded, available individuals willing to be shaped, molded, and carved by His hands."

The daily practice of living Christlike lives will help keep us from having our intentions and actions intercepted by the Evil One. Be accurate and keep focused!

I hope one of my quarterbacks is drawn, so the pie will be intercepted before it gets to my face.

—Jim Fallon, Washington and Lee Coach,
on a drawing to determine which player
would throw a pie at him for charity

> "If it's the ultimate, how come they're playing it again next year?"
>
> —**Duane Thomas,** Former Cowboy Running Back, on the Super Bowl

52

The Glory Days

The title of a featured article in the January 8, 2001, issue of *Christianity Today* is "The Glory of the Ordinary." This interesting interview of quarterback Trent Dilfer by Jeff Sellers provides keen insights into the controversy (and sometimes hypocrisy) associated with Christian football players.

Dilfer was drafted by the Tampa Bay Buccaneers as the sixth player selected from the highly touted class of 1994. The Bucs had high expectations for the 6'4", 229-pound rookie, and after working through some difficult times, Dilfer eventually led the young franchise to a playoff spot in the 1997 season. Unfortunately, his 1998 campaign was below par, and the Bucs decided to place him in a backup role to Shaun King of Tulane. Finally in 1999 Tampa Bay traded the inconsistent Dilfer to the Baltimore Ravens.

The uncertainty of his status (he worked in a backup role to Tony Banks) and the problems of dealing with a long recovery from torn cartilage in his knee began to wear on Dilfer's spirit. However, even with all the possibility for depression and dissatisfaction, he remained strong and dedicated to the game and to his faith.

As a mature believer, Dilfer has a tremendous sense of humility and perspective in knowing how football fits into the scheme of things: "I'm not a football player who happens to do Christianity. I'm a Christian that just happens to be an NFL player," he says. His observations of many "Christian athletes" in the league is that, just like in the real world, there is a significant difference between those who are truly committed to the principles of their faith and those who just wish to give a "nod to God."

In his quest to land a starting position, Dilfer remained patient and faithful. He prayed that the Holy Spirit would allow him to have an attitude of joy and peace in the midst of his setbacks. During even this challenging time he wanted to be used of God to encourage others on his team who were going through their own difficulties.

Throughout the 2000 season Dilfer continued to back up the struggling Tony Banks. The Ravens defense was so awesome that the lifeless offense could somehow still win games. Midway through the season, Coach Brian Billick had had enough. Playoff hopes were forming, and he needed a quarterback that could lead the Ravens to a berth in the Super Bowl. Dilfer got his shot to perform because Banks was having extreme difficulty with control and interceptions.

To most critics' amazement, Dilfer went on to lead the Ravens to an exciting victory in Super Bowl XXXV. In an industry that is laden with big egos, Dilfer makes genuine humility one of his top spiritual quests, and he did so in his post-game interview. His words were indicative of what he had written earlier in his prayer journal: "Thank you, God, that you are using football as the means to break me so that I may know you better."

Despite his success both on and off the field, Dilfer resists saying that because a high-profile athlete professes Christian faith he will automatically have a winning season. He says, "I don't think that our success level dictates the amount we can glorify God." He maintains, "God calls believers first to be faithful, and secondarily to develop 100 percent of what He has given them—whether they are athletes, business owners, spouses, parents, or in any other vocation."

During his *CT* interview with Jeff Sellers, Dilfer goes on to say, "It's the process more than the product that brings Him [God] glory. When folks are truly searching and looking into people's lives to find answers, where they'll see God is in a consistent life, and in the process, not necessarily the end result or the product."

Dilfer realizes the hypocrisy of some who when winning will stand before the national media to proclaim their Lord but then turn right around and become involved with immoral or illegal activities that dishonor God. He knows the players who during a trying time on the field will blaspheme

God's name without regard to how it impacts viewers or teammates. This is why Dilfer feels that consistency in a faithful walk toward a high calling is something for which each believer should strive: "I believe that I am more motivated professionally than I've ever been because God has given me a certain amount of ability, leadership, and other areas that I am called to develop through His strength. This will naturally help me progress in a successful way."

God has given each of these men unique and special talents that make them football players, but their choosing football as an occupation should not preclude their serving and honoring God with their wholehearted efforts. Dilfer says, "It's a time where God has pulled together a group of men to say, 'Okay, after all that's just been said and done, what is our purpose and what is our perspective on life?' "

Christian athletes who are sincere in their faith will tell you that their praises to God after a hard-fought game are a "natural expression of core beliefs" that guide their daily lives. Dilfer's game-day prayer is always the same: "I need your Spirit to be in total control of my thoughts, actions, emotions, and words." This is a reminder to all of us as to how we should place God at the center of all that we do.

Lord, all of you, none of me.

—*Trent Dilfer*

> "The older you get, the faster you ran when you were a kid."
>
> —**Steve Owen,** Former Giants Coach

53

God's Squad

Football has been in my blood ever since I watched Y. A. Tittle chuck a pass to his tight end, Billy Wilson, back in the early 1950s. The passion, pageantry, and planning associated with this great sport all seem to resonate with my character.

As a young person I would come home from church and immediately put on my football helmet and prepare for the TV game of the week. Because my father worked on Saturdays and got home late in the evenings, there really wasn't much time for us to throw the football around. Sunday's televised game was about the only time we were able to bond around something we both enjoyed. However, it was rare for me to sit through an entire game. My excitement spilled over to our long front yard, where I lived out all my fantasies about someday being an NFL player.

Our neighborhood was primarily made up of girls who were more interested in playing dolls than football. I didn't let it bother me, even though there weren't a bunch of guys to play a pick-up game, even though my front yard had cement walkways running through it, and even though I was not physically suited to play the game.

I would pretend to be an NFL quarterback, taking the ball from center and then dropping back to bomb a pass as far and high as I could throw.

This would give me time to race down to the end of the lawn to make a diving catch—sometimes landing on the lawn and sometimes on the walkways.

It had to look strange for anyone driving by the house to see this skinny young lad playing a one-man football game. The roles of quarterback and receiver were not enough, for who better to do the play-by-play announcing than the same person involved in the game? This would be done with all the sounds and words one could muster at eleven years of age. Then there were the imaginary tackles and kick returns and, of course, the victory celebration after a score. Some days I would come in so exhausted that I would literally have to crawl into bed to recover.

This passion for the game carried over into high school, where my coach told me I was too thin (5'11", 135 pounds) to play—without even checking my skill levels, he told me to go out for the golf team instead. Playing football in Oakland back in the late '50s was nothing short of going into combat: most of the players were guys who'd flunked a grade or two and had full-grown physical maturity; they were big and strong and looked to intimidate any smaller player. Unfortunately, most formations called for two big tight ends and very quick running backs. I, of course, was neither big nor quick.

Utilizing an undersized flanker with good hands was something that hadn't yet reached the high school level; this left me to play off-season pick-up games with many of my varsity friends. When I finally got to college and could actually fill out a large jersey, the only option left was to play intramural sports. This was not really satisfying because most players were neither committed nor passionate about the game. It usually ended up as a party scene with little room for developing game-winning strategies.

Having known and interviewed countless professional athletes, I find that there are four things in common with those who've made it to the big leagues:

(1) *God-given abilities.* One thing that separates a college player from a high school player (and a pro player from a college player) is God-given ability. This includes physical size and maturity as well as basic playing skills and coordination. The refinement of these abilities is a function of the player's commitment and dedication to training and practice (see number 3).

(2) *Opportunity.* The community in which you were raised, the schools you attended, and the coach's decisions to place you in a game at a certain time all factor into the opportunity to perform with the God-given abilities

you have. I'm sure there are former players reading this book who can relate to this point. Part of making a team or moving on to a higher level of play is simply being in the right place at the right time.

(3) *Commitment and dedication.* Greats like Johnny Unitas and Tom Landry wouldn't have made it at even a high school level unless they daily worked at perfecting their skills. Practice, practice, practice is what in part separates the great ones from those who warm the bench. Former coach Jimmy Johnson has proven that an individual's work ethic is supreme: Several times over he traded or released some of the most talented players in the game. These men could play football, but they lacked other essential requirements to play on his teams. According to Johnson, "A player has to be teachable; an unteachable player will be miserable personally and fail the team at crucial moments."

(4) *Encouragement.* I'm convinced that encouragement has to be the most important trait of all. You can lack a little in talent, you can play in a small unknown school, but you will most likely never develop the commitment and dedication you need without someone in the balcony of your heart rooting you on and guiding you to the next opportunity. An encourager is more than just a fan: he is someone who loves you enough to share and care. Encouragers are people who come to your games and lift you up when you're down; they can be coaches, relatives, friends, pastors, or other players. If you think about most Hall-of-Famers, you will usually find one or more significant coaches who helped transform them into being a pro. An encourager is someone willing to spend time in refining and developing abilities and character.

I may have missed the opportunity to become a professional football player, but I didn't miss out on being drafted for the most important team— a team with a mission far greater than any NFL game. It's a team whose members are not always the most visible people on the field or who look the best. They may even lack talent or physical ability. The unique thing about this team is that it doesn't require a person to try out, and it costs nothing to join. The team is of divine inspiration; it's called God's Squad.

Much in the same way a good football player is developed, a God's Squad team member needs an opportunity to commit his allegiance to the team; he needs to be dedicated and passionate about his faith; and he needs to be encouraged and be an encouragement to others.

One thing is lacking from God's football field—there are no benches.

Benches are for folks not playing the game. If you are sincere in your beliefs and dedicated to your faith, you will want to get into the game. When Jesus gave the Great Commission just before He left His disciples, He challenged them and us to join in the battle for souls. It is a call to more than pastors or missionaries; it is a call to all who call themselves *Christians*:

> Then Jesus came to them and said, "All authority in heaven and on earth has been given to me. Therefore go and make disciples of all nations, baptizing them in the name of the Father and of the Son and of the Holy Spirit, and teaching them to obey everything I have commanded you. And surely I am with you always, to the very end of the age." (Matthew 28:18–20)

Jesus tells us to pick up our cross (dedication, faith, commitment, skills, abilities, experience, passion, compassion, and obedience) and follow Him: "If anyone would come after me, he must deny himself and take up his cross and follow me" (Matthew 16:24).

You say, "I can't make His team—I'm not good enough, I'm not successful enough, I haven't completed enough good works." My friend, you don't have to worry. Jesus has enough room on His team for the outcasts, the rejected, and the forsaken: "The Spirit of the Lord is on me, because he has anointed me to preach good news to the poor. He has sent me to proclaim freedom for the prisoners and recovery of sight for the blind, to release the oppressed, to proclaim the year of the Lord's favor" (Luke 4:18–19).

If you're not on His team, you need to be. Join today!

If you're good enough, you're big enough.
        —Woody Hayes, Former Ohio State Coach,
        upon meeting 175-pound Howard "Hopalong" Cassidy

> **"I**f you needed four yards, you'd give the ball to Garrison and he'd get four yards. If you needed twenty yards, you'd give the ball to Garrison and he'd get four yards."
>
> —**Don Meredith** on Walt Garrison

54
Never Doubt

One of the character traits that separates the average football players from the great ones is that internal drive or passion we call determination. The unquantifed feature that causes a runner to keep twisting and churning to gain extra yardage is part of the mystique.

A search of various football annals reveals stories of great comebacks that help us remember certain determined players. Certainly Chicago Bear Walter Payton, Minnesota Viking George Foreman, and more recently San Francisco 49er Jeff Garcia, Oakland Raider Rich Gannon, St. Louis Ram Kurt Warner, and Miami Dolphin Jay Fiedler are among those determined players with huge hearts and large ambition. Each of these professionals earned the respect of fans and fellow teammates the hard way. They were initially passed over and deemed unusable by head coaches and owners.

With so many players in the college draft, it's inevitable that some good players will go unrecognized or even undrafted. Despite the highlight footage, physical testing, and combines where athletes can showcase their talents, some will be missed. To those players who really believe in themselves, being overlooked by an NFL scout isn't the end of the world, but often an opportunity to fuel oneself with even more desire and ambition.

In the 1994 East-West Shrine Game, Jeff Garcia, a little known quarterback from San Jose State, approached Bill Walsh, who earlier that season had publicly likened him to a young Joe Montana. Garcia thanked Coach Walsh for his compliment, and Walsh said, "Son, you are going to win this game and become the MVP." Obviously he saw great potential in the young quarterback, painting a bright future.

The West team trailed 28–7 when Garcia entered in the fourth quarter. Three touchdown passes and a two-point conversion later, they beat the East team 29–28. Earlier in the game the MVP votes had been gathered, and another little known quarterback named Jay Fiedler was selected. But after Garcia's performance a recount was conducted. Fiedler and Garcia were voted co-winners of the coveted prize.

These two quarterbacks still went relatively unnoticed until recently. Both played outside the NFL to earn their way to the big leagues. These expatriate warriors don't have cannon-like arms or flat-out speed; they also lack impressive size and physical strength. However, as the model for the ideal NFL quarterback changed with the more sophisticated West Coast Offense, the need for quarterbacks like Warner, Gannon, Fiedler, and Garcia became more apparent.

Walsh says scouting often fails to reveal what a player truly offers and what teams need most: "Intuition, instinct, and natural competitive zeal are immeasurable traits that only a few players have." With all the tests and assessments conducted on the outside of a man's frame, no one has devised an exam to measure the inside—the heart, the spirit, and the mind.

As Garcia recently said in an interview, "People can't measure your heart. . . . [The real question is,] when accurate, timely decisions have to be made, do [we] do the right thing? I always believed that I had what it takes to be a good NFL quarterback." He went on to say, "When people doubted me . . . [it added] fuel to my desire to be the kind of player that I imagined I could be."

I can identify with the determination of those who seek to find their destiny from within. Upon graduating from high school I was determined to be the first male on either side of my family to graduate from college. While getting my master's degree, I took on a lowly job with a park district and was paid the second-lowest wage of any full-time employee.

Despite my feeble title and responsibilities, I believed with hard work and faith in God I could succeed. My ambition and desire to be among the leaders in the park and recreation industry provided much vision. Within a few short years God allowed me the privilege of succeeding in this venture.

Even in the workplace it becomes a matter of internal drive, commitment, and the encouragement of others while being balanced with faith, family, and humility. For most of us engaged in daily living, life isn't a full-ride scholarship or being selected in the first round of the NFL draft. To most who are successful, life is about utilizing our God-given skills and abilities to the fullest in order to provide a living for our family and to glorify our heavenly Father. I'm convinced that those who are most successful in life and who are rewarded by man and God are people who have their priorities in order and who have a deep and abiding faith in Jesus.

Tucked away in the middle of the Old Testament are First and Second Chronicles, historical books that provide insight into the lives of King David and his son Solomon. In these writings we find words of encouragement that help us to remain determined in our quest for success while balanced in our relationships. Success without God in our lives is a deep grave that knows not the light of joy, peace, and grace.

> Then the Spirit of God came upon Azariah (son of Oded), and he went out to meet King Asa as he was returning from the battle. "Listen to me, Asa! Listen, armies of Judah and Benjamin!" he shouted. "The Lord will stay with you as long as you stay with him! Whenever you look for him, you will find him. But if you forsake him, he will forsake you. For a long time now, over in Israel, the people haven't worshiped the true God and have not had a true priest to teach them. They have lived without God's laws. But whenever they have turned again to the Lord God of Israel in their distress and searched for him He has helped them. In their times of rebellion against God there was no peace. Problems troubled the nation on every hand. Crime was on the increase everywhere. There were external wars and internal fighting of city against city, for God was plaguing them with all sorts of trouble. But you men of Judah, keep up the good work and don't get discouraged, for you will be rewarded." (2 Chronicles 15:1–7 TLB)

For those of us who are facing difficult times, it's good to remember that hard work, determination, and a deep faith in God will sustain us through our challenges.

I've found that prayers work best when you have big players.
—*Knute Rockne*

"**I** have never seen a statue that wouldn't look better with [Don] Shula's head on it."

—**Pete Dexter,** Journalist

55

The Perfect Season

To be perfect in any sport and at any level is remarkable. To have a perfect season in the NFL is nearly impossible. When the Miami Dolphins beat the Washington Redskins by a score of 14–7 in Super Bowl VII to finish up their unblemished season, no one could believe it. Miami's domination in the early 1970s is unparalleled in professional football. It's important to note that their work in achieving their records didn't start in the summer training camp of 1972, but two years earlier.

Norm Evans, president of the Pro Athletes Outreach and former All-Pro right tackle, provided me with some insights into how Miami built such a terrific team: "Our preparation for the Super Bowl run began when Head Coach [Don] Shula and Offensive Line Coach Monte Clark came on board in 1970," states the 6'5", 248-pound former lineman. "Shula knew every aspect of the game and instilled in the men a sound work ethic. He expected greatness and would not settle for mediocrity."

"If a nuclear bomb is ever dropped on this country, the only things I'm certain will survive are AstroTurf and Don Shula" (Bubba Paris, Former 49er Offensive Tackle).

In doing some research on Don Shula, I came across an interesting quote by John Madden that helps us understand the man and his vision: "Shula has

200

won with different teams in different cities," Madden said. "He won in Baltimore with Johnny Unitas at quarterback, and he won there with Earl Morrall at quarterback when Unitas was hurt. Then he took over a team in Miami that had Larry Csonka and Bob Griese, and he won the Super Bowl twice." It wasn't the team as much as it was the system and discipline that Shula brought to the game.

In 1970 when Shula arrived on the scene and the players finally came to camp after a difficult labor dispute, he demanded four-a-day workouts so that the players would make up for lost time. No team has ever had more workouts than the 1970 Dolphins. It was expected that each player would not only know his responsibilities on each play but also each of his teammates' assignments. Shula felt this would build accountability and unity.

Additionally, the gifted head coach hired a psychologist to put everyone through detailed testing. "The entire team was locked up for four hours taking various tests," says Evans. The results showed that the Miami Dolphins were a collection of some of the most highly motivated guys in the league.

In order for a great team to be developed, Coach Shula had to take advantage of this individual professional pride and encourage players to help one another become even greater. Shula realized that the team was never going to be better than its weakest link; therefore, each player needed to help and support every other player.

Shula and Clark began an intense program that built a real *esprit de corps* among the players. Evans recalls, "Coach Clark insisted upon the offensive line hanging out together during our off times. He believed that once we got to really know and respect each other, we wouldn't want to let the other guy down."

According to Evans, "Coach Monte built pride, confidence, poise, and a very strong work ethic among the linemen that soon became the standard for the entire team." When the media tried to develop a controversy among the players and the fans about the playing time Jim Kiick and Mercury Morris got, the team stood firm on unity.

Evans states, "The Christians on the team were important to building this unity. They dedicated themselves to modeling harmony and respect. Even the non-chapel guys liked the idea that each man honored and respected his fellow teammates. So we were a very tight group."

When you study game films from that perfect season, you can see the intensity and pride each player had in his performance. They worked together as a finely tuned machine. The team's cohesiveness and unity allowed them to make the most of each play.

Evans says, "We were so good that many of Griese's play calls were made on the line of scrimmage after he quickly evaluated the defense alignment. The offensive players made their individual adjustments as the cadence came down from the All-Pro quarterback."

In 1972 the bench strength, the fact that the team was fundamentally sound, and the excellent physical conditioning proved too much for all their opponents. They won every game they played. Also, despite the fact that the defense had two All-Pro performers in middle linebacker Nick Buoniconti and safety Dick Anderson, the media called it the "No-Name Defense." This unique group truly played as a team.

Over the past several years I have talked with many coaches and players about their concern for the lack of focus and a good work ethic among a few of their teammates. It's difficult for this author to believe that someone could receive millions of dollars for playing football and then, once their contract is signed, slack off to the point of embarrassment. Another disappointment is how a few players risk the team's future because they want to indulge themselves in reckless and illegal behavior.

Unfortunately, human nature being what it is, some guys believe the prima-donna persona that got them by in college will lead them to victory in the pros. Others believe too much in their own game-time abilities and don't feel they need to reach for the next level of conditioning during practice. I'm also unimpressed with the know-it-all attitude demonstrated by some players during critical meetings.

And then there are those who really believe they are perfect; they feel invincible and are cantankerous about how the game is played. However, God's Word tells us that none of us are without flaws: "If we claim to be without sin [perfect], we deceive ourselves and the truth is not in us" (1 John 1:8).

As good as the 1972 Dolphins were, they weren't perfect. Passes were missed, blocks fell short, fumbles were made, and handoffs were muffed. In fact, Norm Evans tells me that the 1973 Dolphin team that lost two games was an even better and stronger unit than the 1972 perfect-season group.

Just as in football, if we deny the failures of the past there is no way we can become better for the future. The Christian life is not about rules and regulations, liturgy and decrees, but about a love relationship with Jesus

Christ. If we really care about someone, our behavior will be so modified that it will honor those whom we love.

When Coach Monte Clark motivated his linemen to get to know one another in a more personal way, the men responded with greater respect for him and for one another. So it is in the Christian experience—once we honor God and His presence in our lives, the more we will want to serve, obey, and love Him. And once we have done that, God wants us to move forward with a new awareness and personal expectation regarding our performance (Philippians 3:13–14).

The freedom of our faith is the grace of a loving God who forgives us our sins. In order for a perfectly holy and righteous God to see us as pure and worthy, it took the supreme sacrifice of His perfect Son on Calvary's cross to provide the ultimate sacrifice for our guiltiness. Unlike a coach who sees the imperfections of each player, when God looks down upon us He sees us through the sacrifice of His Son as if we were perfectly pure.

O Lord, you bless the righteous.

—*Psalm 5:12*

> **"P**laying quarterback is like being in a street fight with six guys, and everybody's rooting for the six."

> —**Dan Pastorini,** Former Oiler Quarterback

56

The Field General

What makes a great quarterback? A former coach with the University of Miami tells us, "Having a pro offense with great receivers but no first-rate quarterback is like having a new limousine with a chimpanzee at the wheel."

The majority of decisions made by a quarterback occur in three-second intervals. That is the time a passer usually has from the moment he takes the snap from the center, hurries back a few yards, searches for a receiver, and fires the ball at a moving target.

To be consistently successful at this day after day and to compete at the NFL level, a quarterback needs several skills and talents. Certainly having a strong and accurate arm is important—he must be able to fling the ball from various positions and for distances up to sixty or seventy yards. He also must have good rhythm and footwork to avoid those blitzing linebackers and safeties. Most quarterbacks who last more than a few years are nimble and agile when it comes to scampering away from trouble. Good footwork is about rhythm and selected movement. Having the right balance and dexterity are key to being effective in gaining more time through scrambling.

A good sense of timing is also critical. My friend Rich Gannon tells me, "You've got to have a game clock going in your head. Everything you do must be totally reactive because you just don't have the time to really think things through during the heat of the battle."

Decision-making is another key. I can think of several quarterbacks drafted recently who were great college quarterbacks, had very strong arms, and were big strapping guys who are now pumping gas or stocking shelves at a mini-mart because they lacked the ability to make good and quick decisions during the course of the game. When you consider what made smaller guys like Montana, Young, Unitas, Tittle, Starr, or Staubach great, you don't immediately think about a big powerful quarterback who can chuck the ball a mile. No, you think of a good decision maker—a guy who can call the right play at the right time; a guy who can anticipate and make quick adjustments to compensate for the defensive play of his opponent.

Finally, an NFL quarterback needs to be a leader. Someone once said, "Leaders are not those who strive to be first but those who are first to strive and who give their all for the success of the team. True leaders are first to see the need, envision the plan, and empower the team for action. By the strength of the leader's commitment, the power of the team is unleashed."

When you see a team struggling, it is most likely because there is a lack of good leadership in some facet of the game. It could be that a team has awesome leadership with the offense but lacks a true leader on the defensive side of the ball. Despite a number of marquee players, good management in the front office, a great quarterback, and vocal fans, without on-the-field leadership the defense and the special teams will struggle. Any championship team has outstanding men who can step up and take on the leadership role— they become field generals. Marian Anderson of the *New York Times* once said, "Leadership should be born out of the understanding of the needs of those who would be affected by it."

Perhaps the single most important trait of a great quarterback and a great man of God is knowing the hearts of the people he is leading. It is a wise football player and servant of God who shows compassion and displays understanding. A person will generate enormous effort when he knows he is respected, loved, and cared for.

Scripture calls men to be leaders in our homes, in our workplaces, and in our churches. To be leaders we must first test our own hearts for purity, righteousness, and obedience. Then we must be willing and fit to lead by example and model the principles of God's Word.

Be a leader, my friend.

The quality of a man's life is in direct proportion to his commitment to excellence, regardless of his chosen field of endeavor.

—Vince Lombardi

57

The Zebras

Many people have been a witness to an event that required them to share their perspective and testimony on the details surrounding it. Sometimes our evaluation and observations serve as conclusive evidence in order to either convict or release a person from court action. In some cases millions of dollars are awarded to an individual because of the explanation of witnesses.

According to *Webster's*, a witness is an observer, onlooker, bystander—a person who saw and can give a firsthand account of something. In football the witnesses are the officials, a.k.a. the Zebras, who are charged by the NFL to enforce the rules and regulations governing game play.

To the casual observer the officials seem to be part of the landscape; someone to place the ball at the correct spot on the field. If your favorite team receives a questionable penalty, then you see the Zebras as a nuisance or a distraction. Much like the NFL players themselves, professional officials are selected based upon their experience and knowledge of the game. They are chosen because of their unbiased approach to making correct calls during critical situations.

My friend Steve Wilson, a pastor in Spokane, Washington, is an NFL umpire (#29) who weekly can be found in his front-row seat next to the middle linebacker. After interviewing Steve, my perspective of officiating changed drastically. Now I'm extremely impressed with the depth of understanding and anticipation an NFL official must have to be effective.

I learned that each official has specific tasks and responsibilities associated with his position. Being in the right spot at the right time is critical to good play-calling and to one's own survival. If a Zebra happens to daydream on a play where the tight end is crossing through his area, he may find the trailing linebackers running right over him.

There are a total of seven officials on the field. The *referee* stands somewhere behind the offensive backfield and is in charge of the officiating crew. The *umpire* stands behind the defensive line and calls any infractions in that area of the field. There is a *head linesman* and a *line judge* that stand at opposite ends of the line of scrimmage and are responsible for tracking the forward progress of the ball, plus keeping track of the downs as well as yardage needed for a first down. The head linesman and line judge are also the official timekeepers. The *field judge* stands behind the secondary and specifically watches punts, kickoffs, and downfield plays. Finally, the *back judge* and the *side judge* keep an eye on the secondary for any infractions.

Each official must be completely familiar with the players and their assignments. Most NFL officials have served for decades at the high school or college level before entering the ranks of the pros. After officiating in college they must have professional experience with either the Canadian or European league before the NFL will consider them.

"Officials are the only guys who can rob you and then get a police escort out of the stadium" (Rob Bolton, Former Brown Defensive Back).

According to Steve Wilson, "The league asks us to concentrate seven to ten seconds at a time, looking for anything that is outside the scope of common play. Our goal is to allow the players to play their game while being able to totally describe everything we see in the area of our responsibility at any given time." In the truest sense of the word, Steve and his fellow officials are witnesses.

One of Wilson's favorite stories deals with a young middle linebacker who was extremely talented and very aggressive: "The teams had been very verbal with one another during the contest," he recalls. "The quarterback called a screen, and the middle linebacker read it all the way. He slipped past the blockers and sought out the back that had his gaze fixed on the ball that was slowly drifting his way. With all the power the linebacker could muster he hit the running back just as the ball arrived." Still recalling the event, Steve described the crash of the two gladiators:

They hit so hard that the running back's helmet flew off and rolled for several yards. The middle linebacker jumped up and started yelling profanities at the disabled player lying on the ground in a daze. It was clear that he was trying to totally intimidate the hurt man and his teammates.

About the time they went to commercial break for the injury timeout, I asked the middle linebacker to clean up his language. I pointed to my lapel mike and reminded him that everything he had said went out over the broadcast and was potentially influencing the audience, including kids and maybe even his family. I reminded him that he was an example, a witness, to others.

With a sheepish look, he grabbed my lapel, held the microphone close to his mouth, and shouted, "Mama, I'm sorry; I'm sorry, Mama!"

In addition to these general uses, the word "witness" is also used in connection with the distinctively Christian message of the Bible. God witnesses to the believer about His assurance of salvation: "The Spirit Himself bears witness with our spirit that we are children of God" (Romans 8:16 NASB). The Bible also declares that God has not left *us* without a witness—the Holy Spirit (Acts 14:17). The believer's life and words serve as a witness to the world. Sometimes this witness is represented in our language, our actions, or our deeds, as well as our attitudes. Most effectively, it is a positive combination of all these things.

Francis of Assisi once said, "Preach the gospel at all times. And, when necessary, use words." This is a tremendous reminder to all of us that our actions and attitudes speak much louder than what we say.

The Christian life is about imitating the character of God in every action and attitude. If we are that kind of witness, we will surely impact people with a love, grace, and mercy that transcend the common boundaries of understanding.

You will receive power when the Holy Spirit comes on you; and you will be my witnesses in Jerusalem, and in all Judea and Samaria, and to the ends of the earth.

—*Acts 1:8*

Chapter

8

Post-Game Wrap-up

Immediately after Kurt Warner and the Rams' victory in Super Bowl XXXIII, an interviewer said, "Kurt, first things first—tell me about the touchdown pass to Isaac [Bruce]." Warner responded, "Well, first things first, I've got to thank my Lord and Savior up above— Thank you, Jesus!"

—Kurt Warner

Super Bowl XXXIII MVP

"**T**exas Stadium has a hole in its roof so God can watch his favorite team play."

—**D. D. Lewis**, Former Cowboy Linebacker

58

It's About Character

Our ministry is regularly involved in providing spiritual messages and outdoor skills training to many who attend our conferences and retreats. We count it a privilege to speak on a variety of subjects, including the importance of building great character.

The National Football League has recently been focusing on improving the character of its coaches and athletes. Several programs have been developed to help teams cope with improper behavior and destructive personal attitudes that affect the reputation of the league.

From a Christian perspective, we are directed by Scripture to continually look for ways to encourage, assist, inspire, and devote ourselves to others. If we truly love others the way we want to be loved, we are doing the will of our Lord. When we model a Christlike love to others, we testify to the character of God living within us. The old expression "More is caught than taught" is true. Discipleship is about presenting a consistent testimony through our actions, attitudes, and words. Remember, our conduct is a direct revelation of our character.

There have been precious few folks who have impacted my life by demonstrating a genuine and consistent Christlike love. Recently, one of my role models went to be with the Lord. Both in his public and private life we saw evidence of his great character.

It was interesting to see the numerous reports and commentaries associated with this man's words and work. Few editorials I read discussed his many worldly accomplishments, but many underscored his courage and integrity. This legendary Hall-of-Fame coach left a legacy of love and encouragement to his players, fans, and the many community organizations he fostered. Tom Landry was a giant of a man whose character and integrity were unquestionable.

Again, despite all his accomplishments in football, after he died the media's primary focus was upon his outstanding character—his good report. Having solid character means that one has a sound moral, ethical, and spiritual undergirding that rests on truth, that reinforces a life, and that resists the temptation to compromise.

Coach Landry's life was not void of errors or confusion, but it was a life of focus and conviction. A pastor friend of mine once asked Landry why he wasn't in the bidding war for a certain All-Pro athlete who had stated he wanted to be a Cowboy. The coach's response was predictable: "The man lacks character. I don't want players who are so full of themselves that they can't be a team player."

Jesus felt very strongly about the issue of character. In Matthew 5 we read His famous Sermon on the Mount; one of the purposes for this message was to communicate the requirements for a godly character (to be "like Him"). To be faithful, committed disciples with honor and virtue, Jesus asked His followers to receive and act upon the "declarations of blessedness." It is only after a disciple becomes humble, compassionate, meek, merciful, kind, pure in heart, and a peacemaker that he can be "the light of the world" and "the salt of the earth"—a role model. Read the declarations on Christ's magnificent teachings and ask yourself: Are you the role model God intends you to be?

You have to know when and how to go down. The key is to have a fervent desire to be in on the next play.

—Jim Zorn, Former Seahawk Quarterback

> "**E**arl Campbell may not be in a class by himself, but whatever class he's in, it doesn't take long to call the roll."
>
> —**Bum Phillips**

59

My MVP

Every year a few dozen professional football players from each conference (National and American) are selected to compete in the Pro Bowl. The starting AFC QB for the 2001 Pro Bowl was thirteen-year veteran Rich Gannon of the Oakland Raiders. (He repeated this honor in 2002.) By the end of the first quarter, Gannon had thrown for 164 yards, including two TDs. His performance testifies to his God-given abilities, mature leadership skills, strength of character, and perseverance. He was unanimously selected as the game's MVP.

As we look through the Bible there are a number of "MVPs" that stand out even more than the great accomplishments of a thousand football stars. Surrounding the remarkable stories and prophecies related to Christ's life is a collection of biblical characters whose lives and testimonies are riveted with incidents that depict integrity.

One of my favorite role models is Daniel. The Babylonian captivity set the stage for a truly uncommon display of integrity and valor from Daniel and his three friends. Despite tremendous adversity, they persevered and kept the faith. They trusted God for deliverance and obeyed His commands.

With adversity as a backdrop, Daniel, Shadrach, Meshach, and Abednego developed a godly character that impressed all who observed their struggles. Their main priority was to serve their God with humility, honor, integrity, and fidelity. When King Nebuchadnezzar offered the best food to these committed Jews, they politely refused the enticement that conflicted with God's teachings. They drew the line and took a stand on biblical principle. That is godly character.

Accepting the king's rations and lifestyle would have defiled them, according to Hebrew law. Daniel and his pals knew that standing on truth would sometimes put a person at odds with those in authority. But they were so committed to being obedient to God's Word they respectfully declined the king's offers.

When we take a stand for kingdom principles, God's favor is our reward and blessing. For example, "Noah found favor in the eyes of the Lord" and was spared the ravages of the flood (Genesis 6:8 NASB). "Joseph found favor in His sight" (Genesis 39:4 NASB) and was elevated to prominence in Egypt (see also Exodus 11:3; 12:36). When Daniel and his associates chose to obey God by not defiling themselves with the king's diet (Daniel 1:8), they demonstrated brave courage and noble integrity.

Today God's favor is the special blessing He grants to His children when we take that difficult stand against the things we know are wrong. Remember,

No temptation has seized you except what is common to man. And God is faithful; he will not let you be tempted beyond what you can bear.

—1 Corinthians 10:13

60

Who's to Blame?

Anyone even casually acquainted with professional football is aware of how the various teams celebrate a score. Some squads have the entire offensive line performing a choreographed routine around the person scoring the touchdown. Some agile players enjoy stuffing the ball over the goalpost crossbar as a way of commemorating their victory. Many flamboyant receivers or running backs perform a personalized dance.

For every offensive celebration there is equal disappointment demonstrated by the opposing defense. The lists of potential excuses are many: someone called the wrong alignment, a critical block or tackle was missed, or maybe a defensive player was simply physically mismatched with his opponent. Equally embarrassing can be the way players respond to the problem. Some will hang their heads and walk dejectedly off the field. Others might literally point the fickle finger of blame at someone else. Sometimes players run off the field to yell at a coach or another player.

Most recently, it has been the custom of embarrassed athletes to literally point the finger of blame on themselves. It is as if they purposely move into an open area of the field and begin head-nodding while pounding their chest as if to say, "It's me! I'm the one to blame!"

However, for a Christian, confession is the first step toward defeating the issue of blame or, in this case, sin. Sometimes the hardest part of dealing with a problem is admitting that you have one. People naturally want to deny responsibility for their failings. Some wish to blame their behavior on bad parenting, the culture in which they were raised, the lack of a proper education, or even that somehow God is against them.

Confession, though, is simply agreeing with God about our sin. It affirms our dependence on a forgiving, merciful Lord who can deal with our failures in a righteous way. By confessing, we restore God's blessing upon our lives.

God's people have always recognized the importance of confession. David acknowledged to Nathan the prophet, and then to God, "I have sinned against the Lord" (2 Samuel 12:13 NASB). As we saw earlier, when Isaiah saw the holiness of God in a vision he declared, "Woe is me, for I am ruined! Because I am a man of unclean lips, and I live among a people of unclean lips" (Isaiah 6:5 NASB). Even Daniel, who had tremendous integrity, confessed his sin: "I was speaking and praying, confessing my sin and the sin of my people Israel and making my request to the Lord my God for his holy hill" (Daniel 9:20).

Ongoing confession of sin to God distinguishes a mature believer. Those who claim to be believers but who refuse to confess their sins deceive themselves (1 John 1:8) and make God a liar (1 John 1:10). Next time you feel like pointing at someone else about a problem, make sure you first consider what sin exists in your own life. As Jesus reminds us, "Why do you look at the speck of sawdust in your brother's eye and pay no attention to the plank in your own eye?" (Matthew 7:3).

If we claim we have not sinned, we make him out to be a liar and his word has no place in our lives.

—1 John 1:10

"The New York Jets should trade their playoff spot to the Seattle Seahawks for an offense to be named later."

—Dave Anderson, Sports Columnist

61

"Mr. Bob" Goes to New York

In their excellent article titled "Absolutely Intense," as seen in the November issue of *Sharing the Victory* (published by the Fellowship of Christian Athletes), Allen Palmeri and Joan Bustos write about the passion and focus of the Jets' head coach, Herman Edwards.

Contained within this work is some revealing material about what shaped the life of this prestigious NFL coach. As a young high school and college player, Edwards was a cocky, brash athlete with a big Afro and a bigger ego. His hard-hitting style of play was second only to his quickness and confidence.

As a cornerback he patterned his speed and attitude after Dallas Cowboys All-Pro wide receiver Bob Hayes. Edwards insisted that coaches liken him to the world-class Olympian and call him "Mr. Bob." Unlike the road Bob Hayes took to finally seeking God, Herman "Mr. Bob" Edwards had a more direct approach to finding true victory and peace in his life.

Edwards was drafted by the Philadelphia Eagles and ended his career with many interceptions, starting 135 games as an Eagle and never missing a practice at any level of football. "I came to work every day," he says. Even so, his greatest victory came when his teammate and friend Randy Logan influenced him to stand up for Jesus Christ.

As Edwards went into coaching with the Kansas City Chiefs, the "Mr. Bob" persona was dropped. The smug personality he had before receiving Christ was put aside for a confident and self-assured spirit that impacted his fellow coaches and players.

As an encourager, Edwards helped Tampa Bay cornerback John Lynch get to the Pro Bowl. "This is a great man of character, a man who, when he commits himself to something, it's all-out," Lynch says. According to Lynch, Coach Edwards always told the players, "Work hard, be honest, and do your best. Autograph your performance. Put it in the record books!"

In 1996 Edwards left the Chiefs to take a position in Tampa Bay under his longtime mentor and friend Tony Dungy. Dungy implanted great wisdom, supreme confidence, and more mental toughness into Edwards' life. Accepting a job as head coach on the world's largest stage—as Edwards later did in New York City, for the Jets—requires a special inner sturdiness. He was selected for the job because his passion and work ethic are indicative of the profile it takes to be a winner. The difference between Edwards and a few other hardworking coaches is that he is willing to stand up and be accountable for his faith in Jesus Christ.

Herman Edwards actually likes the toughness of standing for Christ in the public arena, and he accepts the reality that there is ridicule awaiting anyone who takes this position as a believer in Jesus. He describes his feelings this way: "You open yourself up for it, but that's okay. I like it, because it really puts a foundation under what I believe."

Few things are more encouraging than watching a prominent Christian remain faithful under fire. Whether it's the president of the United States, a great community leader, or the head coach of an NFL team, the effect is the same. Someone has said, "The furnace of individual trials and persecution is designed by God for the purpose of melting away the debris of our personal lives and purifying what is left." Edwards obviously knows that, or he would not embrace the testing of his faith.

When Edwards shares his life and testimony, he usually quotes Proverbs 22:1: "It's better to have a good name than all the riches in the world" (author's paraphrase). While diligently striving to win a second world championship for the Jets, he has remained under control and steadfast to the principles found in God's Word.

A good name and a respectable reputation have helped Edwards walk the "unseen journey" of faith. Most coaches continually ask their teams to provide maximum effort and intense focus while playing with great passion. They bark at their teams when a player loses control and gets a penalty. Yet many passionate coaches fail to realize the importance of modeling the same principles of self-discipline they try to coach into their players.

Behavior and language that are on the verge of losing control don't model an appropriate attitude. I have seen in my experience that on a team of fifty-three players, 20 to 40 percent of the guys attend chapel and *want* to be associated with Christians. While playing to win, those players who are really committed to their faith desire to model Christlike behavior.

When a coach loses his temper or exhibits inappropriate action or blasphemous language, it drives a penetrating wound into the soul of a believer. I've talked to players who tell me their attitudes and actions on the field are in part a result of how a coach manages his tongue. It's not about judging or condemning coaches who seem to think that being verbally abusive is a way to motivate players. It's also not about being perfect, for we all have sinned and fall short of God's standard (Romans 3:23). While grace should be the reality that most occupies a believer's spirit, it is important for others to *see* the wisdom found in the style and management success that marks a coach like Herman Edwards.

Edwards is no less effective because he models his faith. A former teammate who is now an FCA urban director in Philadelphia states, "Herman is a class act. [But] is he intense and effective? Absolutely!"

Let no corrupt communication proceed out of your mouth, but that which is good to the use of edifying, that it may minister grace unto the hearers.

—*Ephesians 4:29* KJV

"**L**ast week on a television show I said, 'Some people don't know a football from a banana.' The next morning a local distributor sent me a huge crate of bananas. This week I'm going to say, 'Some people don't know a football from a Mercedes.'"

—John McKay, Former Buccaneers Coach

62

What's in a Name?

If you hang around folks who like to talk about football, it won't take long before they will mention the nicknames of their favorite stars. To those less passionate about the game and who might observe this dialogue, it's as if some weird charismatic spirit takes over the more animated fans—their language becomes coded and mixed with abbreviations and nonsensical words. Terms like blitz, red-dog, cover-man, TD, red zone, rollout, under center, screen, and wideout make little sense outside of a football conversation.

Characters who have unique nicknames like The Gipper, Papa Bear, Slingin' Sammy, Golden Boy, Mercury, Bum, Boomer, The Snake, Mr. Hollywood, Neon, Hacksaw, Ickey, Deacon, The Galloping Ghost, Broadway Joe, Whiteshoes, The Zonk, The Fridge, Mean Joe, and Dandy Don are etched in the vivid memory of any fan over fifty years of age.

Each of these names means something to pundits of the game. Most often, it's local sportswriters or teammates that give a person his nickname. Some are earned, while others are a reflection of playing style or persona. You could almost fill a notebook of monikers when listening to ESPN's Chris

Berman narrate video clips. His enthusiastic style helps fans identify the person or experience with unusual adjectives and graphic nomenclatures.

What is the name that is above every name? Recently I was reading a devotional by John MacArthur that helped clarify my thinking on this question. "To be consistent with Scripture, it has to be a name that goes beyond merely distinguishing one person from another," states MacArthur. "It has to be a name that describes Christ's nature—revealing something of His inner being."

Throughout Scripture we see Christ distinguished in many ways. Isaiah foretold that He would be known as "Wonderful Counselor, Mighty God, Everlasting Father, Prince of Peace" (Isaiah 9:6). In the New Testament we see Him called "the bread of life" (John 6:35), "the good shepherd" (John 10:11, 14), "the way and the truth and the life" (John 14:6), or "the resurrection and the life" (John 11:25).

A nickname in Scripture indicates the depth of one's relationship to God. The very character of God is such that He requires almost three dozen names to help us understand the various facets of His identity.

When God established His covenant with Abram, He changed his name to "Abraham" ("father to many nations," Genesis 17:5). God's special relationship with Jacob required that he be renamed "Israel" ("the one who struggles with God," Genesis 32:22–32). Jesus took a common fisherman named Simon, who became a rock of truth, and renamed him Peter ("rock," Matthew 16:18).

As the character of Christ grew, God went beyond the common or ordinary in the term that would most describe His only begotten Son. Scores of men in history have been named Jesus. God knew the name "Jesus" alone would not distinguish His precious Son. The only name mentioned in Philippians 2:9–11 (NASB) that is above every name is *Lord*. Paul tells us, "God highly exalted Him, and bestowed on Him the name which is above every name, that at the name of Jesus every knee should bow ... and that every tongue should confess that Jesus Christ is Lord."

The name "Lord," *kurios*, is a Greek New Testament term for the description of God as sovereign ruler. It signifies kingship based on power and authority. The name *Lord* as described in the New Testament denotes the God-man Jesus.

Is Jesus the Lord of your life? The greatest "nickname" I've ever heard is *Christian*. A Christian is a disciple of the Lord. To receive Jesus as Lord means that you submit to His sovereignty and authority in your life. As long as He is the playmaker, we need not worry about making the wrong decision.

All rational beings will acknowledge Christ as Lord.
—Dr. John MacArthur

> "He was the only man I ever saw who ran his own interference."
>
> —**Steve Owen,** on Bronko Nagurski

63

The Bootleg

In hunting, the essence of being stealthlike is to move through the woods undetected. To do this you need to be conscious of the environment, to be nimble in your movements, and to mask your presence with the proper camouflage clothing and game scents. A good deer hunter must go where the deer are. To be successful he must outsmart the old buck by fitting in and not worrying the animals with his looks, scent, or movement.

In a similar manner, a good quarterback camouflages his handling of the ball in such a way as to confuse his opponents about its location. His experience of knowing exactly when to fake the handoff for maximum concealment will help confound the opponent. When a quarterback fakes to a back and then tucks the ball alongside his body and dashes for yardage himself, it is called a "bootleg."

A "naked bootleg" isn't something a guy does with no clothes on but is an event when, after making the fake handoff, the QB runs with the ball in a counter-direction to the flow of his blockers. He is virtually on his own. If you have an extremely reactive defense that is following the initial movement of the backs and blockers, they will automatically pull themselves out of the play as they follow the decoys. This will often leave the quarterback moving toward the opposite sideline from the flow with the ball carefully concealed.

The same type of fake to a running back is followed by a drop-back pass—this is called a "bootleg pass" or a "play-action pass." This deceptive move usually freezes the defensive linemen and linebackers for a second or two before they realize that the quarterback still has the ball. These concealed plays are designed to throw the defense into one pattern and then suddenly change your attack. In many cases a defense can't adjust quickly enough to stop the advance of the ball.

It's critical that everyone involved in the deception plays out his part. The running back must "sell" the event by assuming to protect the ball while in the running position. The back must act like he has surrounded the ball with the hope of bashing into the line. The linemen must move in the appropriate direction as if the back was running through his designated gap. To open up areas of the field beyond the line of scrimmage with the bootleg or naked bootleg, the receivers must run deep patterns that take the defensive backs out of the picture.

A successful team knows how and when and where to hide the ball. While this might be an effective strategy for hunting or football, it has its problems when it comes to sharing our faith:

> God did not give us a spirit of timidity, but a spirit of power, of love and of self-discipline. So do not be ashamed to testify about our Lord, or ashamed of me his prisoner. But join with me in suffering for the gospel, by the power of God, who has saved us and called us to a holy life—not because of anything we have done but because of his own purpose and grace. (2 Timothy 1:7–9)

Is your faith camouflaged? Some Christians tend to conceal their faith so much that they become spiritually invisible to others, even their own families. Some don't want to stand out in the corrupt marketplace of life by treating others with a heart of service or staying clear of jokes and materials promoting pornography. They don't relish upholding principles of truth and fairness when it costs or keeping to values of integrity when the trend is going the opposite direction.

Ultimately this strategy of concealment is a poor witness (testimony) to others about our faith. The apostle John in his third epistle tells us, "Dear friend, do not imitate what is evil but what is good. Anyone who does what is good is from God. Anyone who does what is evil has not seen God" (3 John 11).

We must let others see the love, joy, peace, comfort, strength, and assurance that only Christ can provide. A person filled with these traits is overflowing with God's character and will stand out from the apathetic crowd.

If we stand out from society for the right reasons, we can become a real encouragement to others. People will ask you for your advice and opinions; they will seek your support and wisdom. You will find that others will want to be like you—this is the essence of discipleship, the idea of imitating the Christlike character you see in people and then passing that along to others by the way you live your life.

The writer of Hebrews puts it this way: "Remember your leaders, who spoke the word of God to you. Consider the outcome of their way of life and imitate their faith" (13:7). Don't conceal your faith like a hidden football on a good bootleg. Try to share your faith in a loving way so that others will want to tackle the truth.

I haven't hit him yet, and now I never will.

—Doug Buffone,
after hearing about the retirement
of scrambler Fran Tarkenton

64

Catch the Ball

Long before I arrived in this world, a tall but slender man named Don Hutson joined the Green Bay Packers. Hutson was from the University of Alabama, where he had been an All-American on his senior team, a Rose Bowl winner. His patented catching style eventually placed him in the NFL Hall of Fame.

For eleven seasons Hutson led the league in scoring. Years after he retired his legacy still prevailed. Talk of his precise routes and game-winning catches still lingered in locker room conversations among defensive players. After looking at some old game footage, aspiring Packer cornerback Jess Whitten-ton said, "Hutson had moves that some of the receivers around now haven't even thought of yet. He was great."

Perhaps the most unusual praise of Hutson's talent came from baseball Hall-of-Famer Willie Mays:

I saw Hutson in the movies once. I saw how he caught the ball and stopped real fast. I told myself that if he could do that with a football, I could do it with a baseball. I went out and ran hard at the fence and stopped. I kept doing it until I could do it well. He'd catch the ball and twist away from a guy going to tackle him. I caught a baseball and twisted away from the fence.

It was Hutson, not the great wide receivers of today, who elevated receiving into an art form. Don Hutson still holds several NFL records and is considered the ultimate precision-pattern receiver.

Not only was Hutson agile and cunning, but he also had drive and passion to catch the ball—so much so that he coined the concentrated moment of catching a pass as "looking the ball into your hands." Hutson's size was no factor in how or where he caught the ball. He didn't shy away from crossing over the middle and taking a lick from an angry safety or middle linebacker. Someone once said about him, "It's not the size of the dog in a fight, but the size of the fight in the dog." Don had a mission and a motivation to be the very best . . . and he was.

It is this type of zeal and commitment that helped motivate people like Jerry Rice, who says, "Whenever the ball is in the air, I believe it belongs to me." As we have seen, being a great football player requires enormous effort, focus, passion, and commitment, as well as an inward strength of character. This internal power comes first from recognizing our deficits and shortcomings.

Being a dedicated follower of Jesus also requires tremendous strength of character, and a relationship with God is built first upon acknowledging our inward weaknesses. The apostle Paul said, "If I must boast, I will boast of the things that show my weakness . . . so that Christ's power may rest on me" (2 Corinthians 11:30; 12:9).

As with Paul's thorn in the flesh, our defects are continual reminders of our need for a caring, loving, compassionate, merciful, gracious Savior. In recent discussions with a chaplain who ministers to athletes, he said, "Most of them have an indifference to spiritual matters that keeps them from really exploring the claims of Christ." He went on to say, "Some athletes have learned to block out felt needs, such as pain, so they can concentrate on performing in their sport. Competition has trained athletes to feign strength by denying weakness."

Joe Namath once reported Coach Bear Bryant's response to a teammate's injury: "Nobody ever died of a broken finger!" Some say that men are tough; they can handle their problems. But true strength comes through admitting our inadequacy; it is when we acknowledge our true dependence on our

Creator that we can really find the ultimate strength and power that separates us from the sins and problems of the world. Paul underscores this concept:

I can do all things through Christ who strengthens me.
—*Philippians 4:13* NKJV

"Never let hope elude you. That is life's biggest fumble."

—Bob Zuppke

65

Football and Hope

Next to NASCAR, football ranks as the top spectator sport in the United States. Fans will often debate about whether college football is more exciting than the NFL, or whether Arena football is a real game, or whether another league like the XFL should even exist. After all the arguing settles down we find a slight difference in rules, size of the fields, or the continued rivalry between the AFC and the NFC. But mere tongue exercises do not take away from the unique excitement this sport brings to our culture. There is a vicarious experience that happens to average couch-potato fans who see big, quick, talented men work to a point of near exhaustion in order to move a little air-filled bag of leather up and down a field, mostly oblivious to the pain they are administering to others.

The original rugby/soccer-styled game, later called football, has grown dramatically in its popularity from the early 1890s. Amos Alonzo Stagg, Pop Warner, and other pioneers would probably not recognize today's game. Put the word "football" into your Internet search engine and you'll find hundreds of supportive sites dealing with topics from "Women in Football" to "God and Football."

Twenty-four hours a day, radio and TV sports talk stations beam their messages of hope and doom to all who wish to listen. There are speculators, prophets, reporters, bookies, and stockholders—all of whom consider themselves experts, most of whom think that an athletic supporter is an energetic fan.

Still, with all its adulation and pomp, football is football. It is played one down at a time; often gains are measured one yard at a time. With all the innovation and new technology, the most constant standard found in any huddle, on any bench, and in any locker room remains as it was from the beginning—hope!

A player enters training camp with the hope of making the team. Then he must hope that his skills and knowledge so impress the coaches that he will be selected to be a starter. Once the game starts, the player hopes he can remember all his assignments. Then he hopes his physical and emotional capabilities are up to the challenges and stresses he will face week after week. With each tackle there is the hope that he won't sustain a career-ending injury; even top players are only one play away from retirement.

The hope-filled life of a player continues as he expects to make it to the playoffs, Super Bowl, Pro Bowl, and to repeat all of that the next year. He hopes his patient family will understand that during the season, football has a dominant place in his life.

Hope is defined as "a feeling that what is wanted is likely to happen; desire accompanied by expectation." It is also defined as a trust or reliance upon something. Many NFL or college players have come to realize that at the end of the day there is only one thing that warrants our expectations and will soothe our fears: a relationship with God Almighty. He is the only one that remains constant and the only one in whom we can place our complete trust. In the final analysis, He is our only Hope.

I started this book by acknowledging the plight of our great country. I confessed my hope that those lives and families personally impacted by the events of September 11, 2001, might feel the comfort and peace only the God of all creation can provide. Now it's time to return from that great unknown and often-experienced emotion that only hope brings:

> Today we especially come together . . . to confess our need of God. We've always needed God from the very beginning of this nation, but today we need Him especially. We're facing a new kind of enemy. We're involved in a new kind of warfare, and we need the help of the Spirit of God. The Bible's words are our *hope*: "God is our refuge and strength, an ever present help in trouble. Therefore we will not fear, though the earth

give way and the mountains fall into the heart of the sea" (Psalm 46:1–2, from Billy Graham's message on September 14, 2001).

When Billy Graham spoke at the National Day of Prayer and Remembrance, he reminded the nation that our *hope* is in a caring and loving God. His words encouraged us to remember that there is *hope* for the present and for the future. The *hope* for the present is that we are seeing a nation turning its spirit and its heart back to God.

If you are discouraged, take heart. Look at the benefits that *hope* gives us:

- Hope helps me get started in the right direction: "But those who hope in the Lord will renew their strength. They will soar on wings like eagles; they will run and not grow weary, they will walk and not faint" (Isaiah 40:31).
- Hope helps me overcome obstacles: " 'For I know the plans I have for you,' declares the Lord, 'plans to prosper you and not to harm you, plans to give you hope and a future' " (Jeremiah 29:11).
- Hope helps me keep going: "In this you greatly rejoice, though now for a little while you may have had to suffer grief in all kinds of trials" (1 Peter 1:6).

Problems are inevitable and unexpected. Think about the process of our *hope*:

- We must embrace our problems and face our tribulation: "We also rejoice in our sufferings, because we know that suffering produces perseverance; perseverance, character; and character, hope. And hope does not disappoint us, because God has poured out his love into our hearts by the Holy Spirit, whom he has given us" (Romans 5:3–5).
- We must practice patience and perseverance: "But if we hope for what we do not yet have, we wait for it patiently" (Romans 8:25).
- We must learn the lessons that will help grow our character and witness: "Command those who are rich in this present world not to be arrogant nor to put their hope in wealth, which is so uncertain, but to put their hope in God, who richly provides us with everything for our enjoyment" (1 Timothy 6:17).
- We must enjoy our hope and relish the opportunity to encourage others: "Praise be to the God and Father of our Lord Jesus Christ! In his great mercy he has given us new birth into a living hope through the resurrection of Jesus Christ from the dead" (1 Peter 1:3).

The hectic pace of our modern society often creates more stress, chaos, and confusion than it provides opportunities for a person to contemplate great truths and God's comforting words. I encourage you to spend time in God's great outdoors to experience the peace and quiet needed to restore and renew your body, mind, and spirit. Spend time in God's Word also; your relaxed and calmed mind will settle in on how to live the Christian life more effectively. I trust you will have a hope-filled life, receiving the benefits of a personal relationship with the Lord.

Put your hope in God.

—Psalm 42:5

Sources and Recommended Reading

Anderson, Dave. *The Story of Football* (New York: William Morrow and Company, 1997).

Balzer, Howard. *Sport Snaps—Kurt Warner* (Ballwin, Mo: GHB Publishers, 2000).

Bass, Tom. *Play Football the NFL Way* (New York: St. Martin's Press, 1991).

Bolin, Dan. *Avoiding the Blitz* (Colorado Springs: Navpress, 1998).

Chieger, Bob, and Pat Sullivan. *Football's Greatest Quotes* (New York: Simon & Schuster, 1990).

Dreayer, Barry. *Teach Me Sports* (Los Angeles: General Publishing Group, 1994).

Fisher, Rita McKenzie. *Lessons From the Gridiron* (Portland: New Leaf Press, 1995).

Getz, Gene. *The Measure of a Man* (Gospel Light Publications, 1997).

Hagee, John. *God's Two-Minute Warning* (Nashville: Thomas Nelson, 2000).

Hand, Jimmie. *At the Cross: The Napoleon Kaufman Story* (CWC Publishing, 2001).

Hollander, Zander. *Great American Athletes of the 20th Century* (New York: Random House, 1966).

Jeremiah, David. *The Power of Encouragement* (Eugene, Ore.: Multnomah Publishers, Inc. 1998).

Landry, Tom. *An Autobiography of Tom Landry* (Grand Rapids: Zondervan, 1990).

Liebman, Glenn. *Football Shorts* (Chicago: Contemporary Books, 1997).

———. *2,000 Sports Quips and Quotes* (New York: Gramercy Books, 1993).

MacArthur, John. *Strength for Today* (Wheaton, Ill.: Crossways Books, 1997).

MacDonald, Gordon. *Restoring Your Spiritual Passion* (Nashville, Tenn: Thomas Nelson, 1986).

Oakland Raiders Press Guide, 2001.

Ogilvie, Lloyd. *Twelve Steps to Living Without Fear* (Eugene, Ore.: Harvest House, 1999).

Otto, Jim. *Jim Otto: The Pain of Glory* (Oakland: Sports Publishing Inc., 2000).

Palmeri, Allen. *Absolutely Intense* (Kansas City, Mo.: Sharing the Victory, 2001).

Reich, Frank. TheGoal.com.

San Francisco 49ers Press Guide, 2001.

St. John, Bob. *Landry: The Legend and the Legacy* (Nashville: Thomas Nelson, 2000).

Sanders, Deion. *Power, Money, and Sex* (Nashville: Word, 1999).

Sellers, Jeff. "The Glory of the Ordinary" (*Christianity Today*, Oct. 2001).

Silver, Michael "Raiders of the Lost Arts" (*Sports Illustrated*, Nov. 2001).

Warner, Kurt. *All Things Possible* (Grand Rapids: Zondervan, 2000).

Whittingham, Richard. *The Dallas Cowboys* (New York: Harper & Row, 1981).

Newspapers:

Contra Costa Times
The Sacramento Bee
The Tribune
USA Today

About the Author

Rev. Jim Grassi is an award-winning author, communicator, outdoorsman, and former television co-host. He has presented chapel messages and motivational talks to football teams across the nation. His thoughtful presentations connect with our sports-minded culture. Raised in the San Francisco Bay area, his thirty-five years of experience in the outdoors have given him a unique perspective on working with both amateur and professional athletes.

Grassi is president of the culturally strategic Let's Go Fishing Family Ministries, an organization he founded in 1981. LGFM utilizes outdoor activities to help strengthen families while encouraging personal discipleship. The ministry's full-time team (plus two hundred volunteers) provides instructional programs in wholesome, relaxed settings.

Grassi is also the author of several bestselling books, including *Promising Waters, Heaven on Earth, In Pursuit of the Prize, The Ultimate Fishing Challenge,* and *The Ultimate Hunt. In Pursuit of the Prize* was recognized with the coveted Silver Angel Award for excellence in media.

Grassi has been featured on several television and radio programs, including *The 700 Club, The Carol Lawrence Show, Cornerstone Television, Southern Baptist Television-Cope, Chicago Television 38, The Dick Staub Show, Getting Together, In Fisherman, Fishing Tales, Jimmy Houston Outdoors,* and *Home Life.*

Grassi received his B.S. in Recreation/Park Administration, an M.P.A. from California State University at Hayward, and is ordained by the Evangelical Church Alliance. He and his wife, Louise, make their home in Post Falls, Idaho. They have twin sons, Dan and Tom, in full-time ministry, as well as two precious daughters-in-law, Thelma and Della, and five grandchildren: Dana, Tyler, Maddie, Ruthie, and Danielle.

Making More of Your Pastimes

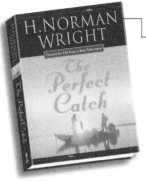
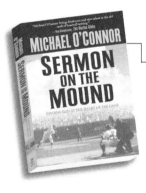